The History Teacher's Handbook

Also available from Continuum

Resources for Teaching History 11–14, Susie Hodge
Resources for Teaching History 14–16, Susie Hodge
100+ Ideas for Teaching History, Julia Murphy

The History Teacher's Handbook

Neil Smith

A companion website to accompany this book is available online at:

http://education.smith.continuumbooks.com

Please visit the link and register with us to receive your password and to access these downloadable resources.

If you experience any problems accessing the resources, please contact Continuum at: info@continuumbooks.com

Continuum International Publishing Group
The Tower Building   80 Maiden Lane, Suite 704
11 York Road   New York, NY 10038
London
SE1 7NX

www.continuumbooks.com

As this book was going to press a new coalition government was making changes within education, so references to the TDA, QCDA and any other governmental website may no longer be coompletely up-to-date.

Resources section

Quick Glossary of Terms © Tabatha Wood
Education and Government © Simon Taylor
Teacher Training © Simon Taylor
Unions © Simon Taylor
Curriculum © Simon Taylor
Subject Associations © Simon Taylor
Exam Boards © Simon Taylor
Media © Simon Taylor
Lesson Planning © Simon Taylor
Inclusion – SEN and other barriers to learning © Simon Taylor
Lesson Plans © Simon Taylor
Other Useful Websites © Simon Taylor
References © Simon Taylor

British Library Cataloguing-in-Publication Data
A catalogue record for this book is available from the British Library.

ISBN: 9781441145345 (paperback)

Library of Congress Cataloging-in-Publication Data
Smith, Neil.
      History teacher's handbook / Neil Smith.
          p. cm. – (Continuum education handbooks)
      Includes bibliographical references.
      ISBN 978-1-4411-4534-5 (pbk.)
    1. History teachers–Training of–United States–Handbooks, manuals, etc.
2. History–Study and teaching–United States–Handbooks, manuals, etc. I. Title.
II. Series.

      LB1582.U6S65   2010
      907.1′073–dc22

                                    2010001028

Typeset by BookEns, Royston, Herts.
Printed and bound in Great Britain by CPI Antony Rowe, Chippenham

Contents

 = also available online

Acknowledgements

In order to draw on good practice in a number of educational contexts, I have discussed many of these ideas with several current and retired history teachers, and the contribution of the following individuals to my research is much appreciated: my colleagues in the History Department at The Manchester Grammar School (MGS); Lucy Merlo, Specific Educational Needs Coordinator at MGS, who kindly reviewed the chapter on accessibility and made several invaluable suggestions; the D13 History set (2009/10) for their fascinating insight into the appeal and uses of history; Caron Walker, Head of History at Baines School, and Toby Miller, Head of History at Fallibroome High School, who both agreed to be interrogated about their respective departmental policies; Nicola Goodwin and Sarah Kay Garside, who both did successful PGCE placements at MGS and provided some useful ideas on creating databases; and Glynn Wales from the History PGCE Department at Durham University, who kindly agreed to trial some of the ideas with his trainees. Of course, responsibility for any errors of fact, judgement or pedagogy is mine alone!

I should also express my sincere gratitude to the plethora of editors who have provided advice, support and forbearance since work on the book began: Christina Garbutt, Melanie Wilson and Ania Leslie-Wujastyk.

Finally, I am most grateful for the love, indulgence and encouragement of Rebecca, Alice, Mollie and Rosy Smith.

Introduction

Is history on the decline?

Anyone reading the newspapers over the last few years would have come across ample evidence of the decline of history as a major subject in the secondary curriculum. Firstly, the Conservative Party obtained data under the Freedom of Information Act which suggested that up to 5 million pupils of school-leaving age had missed out on the opportunity to study history to GCSE since 1997, with one-third of pupils not taking the subject up to the age of 16 in 1998.

Then, a report by the Historical Association, *Findings from the Historical Association survey of secondary history teachers* published in September 2009, appeared to add weight to the Conservative Party's fears about the future of the subject. Based on a survey of over 700 teachers, it claimed that 'many children receive little or no history education after only two years of secondary school', that 11–12-year-olds spend less than an hour a week learning history in a larger number of academies, and that many maintained schools report a fall in the time allocated for the teaching of Key Stage 3 (KS3) history.

According to the report, the main reasons for these trends appear to be:

- Schools adopting a more thematic, humanities-style approach
- A small number of schools delivering a skills-based curriculum, rather than one built around subjects
- An increasing number of schools establishing a 'collapsed' KS3 curriculum, where pupils are allowed to make GCSE choices at the end of Year 8. Whilst history is obviously one of the subjects which can be chosen to study at GCSE, the factors affecting take up at KS4

come into play a year earlier where the KS3 curriculum is condensed into a two-year course. This will also undoubtedly have an impact on the kind of history experienced by pupils in Years 7 and 8. Teachers will be forced either to ignore large sections of the Programme of Study or to offer a very superficial treatment of the various units.
- History is regarded as a difficult subject, with a lot of content to revise.
- Managerial decisions to restrict the time devoted to foundation subjects.

The report also establishes a link between this decline in curriculum time and the falling popularity of the subject at GCSE, where their research supports the figures released under the Freedom of Information Act. Over a period of 14 years, the number of students taking the GCSE history examination has fallen from approximately 40% in 1995 to 30% in 2009.

A common factor in causing the fall-off in numbers is increased competition from subjects perceived to be 'easier', such as PE, or ICT, and from qualifications such as the BTEC offering the equivalent of three or four GCSEs. The recent introduction of diplomas is likely to exacerbate the problem, as less able pupils are pushed towards vocational options, and schools have to coordinate their timetables with neighbouring schools to help deliver some of the diploma courses.

By way of contrast, the status and popularity of history in independent schools remains high. The Historical Association report stated that 97% of independent schools teach history as a discrete subject in Year 7 (compared to 72% of comprehensives and 59% of academies). Most students in the fee-paying sector will sit a GCSE examination in history, and take-up after age 16 is also healthy. Why the difference with the maintained sector?

- More students from independent schools will apply for competitive analysis-based degree courses. History provides an ideal grounding for subjects such as Law.
- The perceived difficult of the subject is an attraction for some pupils within the independent sector.
- Typically, a narrower curriculum is offered, even when broad-based curriculums such as the International Baccalaureate are followed. Competition from other subjects will therefore be less intense.
- The narrower curriculum ensures that pupils are guaranteed more history in their curriculum than their counterparts in the state

sector. In some cases, there was evidence that the amount of time being devoted to history in the independent sector was double the amount provided elsewhere.

What do pupils think about history (and why this is important)?

The irony of this, however, is that other indicators suggest that history is actually in very rude health. A recent Ofsted (2007) report highlighted the quality of teaching performed by history teachers, noting that 80% of lessons observed were either excellent or good (compared to an all subject average of 72%), whilst recent research by Harris and Haydn (2008) highlights the positive impression which the subject makes on young people.

Their survey of over 1700 pupils in Years 7–9 discovered that not only was history a very popular subject, it was *the* most popular 'academic' subject (perhaps inevitably, creative subjects such as PE, art, design and ICT came top), but that its popularity had increased since previous studies. Its popularity was largely attributable to *how* it was taught. The study does not discount the importance of who is teaching it, and what is being taught, but most of the evidence pointed at the teaching approaches as being the critical factor. Unsurprisingly, the majority of respondents expressed a preference for 'active' learning approaches, with role-play/drama and debate the most preferred options. This supports the research carried out by Hattie (2008), outlined later in the book, that whole-class interactive methods have the greatest effect on pupil performance. Although it is difficult to establish a concrete link between active teaching methods and the popularity of the subject, Harris and Haydn's research demonstrates that, when taught well, active approaches make a significant difference to pupil attitudes. If pupils like the subject, then one can assume that they are more likely to be well motivated and focused on academic success.

Why do I need this handbook?

The key point about this and other research into pupil attitudes and performance is that the role of the teacher is vital to pupil enjoyment and performance. Pursuing active approaches is no guarantee of success, if they are done spasmodically or executed poorly. The primary function of this book is to provide history teachers with a broad range of strategies to keep active learning approaches at the forefront of their work. Each chapter combines elements of recent research with 'road-tested' classroom techniques to suggest how you can make your classroom a dynamic and productive learning environment. Advice is given on all aspects of history teaching, from how to plan for successful outcomes and ensure meaningful assessment is carried out, to exciting ways to examine evidence and develop pupil interest outside of the classroom. The chapter on making effective use of ICT to teach history tackles one of the biggest challenges for teachers today: how to ensure new technologies are exploited to improve learning, without allowing the technology to detract from the history being taught. ICT has huge potential for making history exciting and active, but, like any other resource, it has to be used correctly. Standing in front of a PowerPoint presentation for half an hour, or setting the pupils off on a website hunt for the whole lesson, can be as demotivating as providing a list of ten questions from a textbook and telling them to get on with it!

Like all teachers, historians have an increasing responsibility to make the subject accessible to every child. Chapter 4 on inclusion outlines strategies which are designed to make it relevant and accessible to pupils with a range of specific educational needs, which also includes pupils whose first language is not English and those who are regarded as being gifted and talented.

Planning for effective history teaching

1

Bad planning often leads to poor-quality lessons, which in turn are a primary cause of poor behaviour. Whilst good planners can make highly effective teachers, planning by itself cannot transform someone into a superstar in the classroom. This chapter, therefore outlines the qualities of successful teachers and attempts to demonstrate how careful attention to how pupils are going to learn is highly likely to improve both the quality of learning and the level of behaviour.

What is effective teaching?

In order to plan for effective teaching, it might be worth taking a moment to consider what effective teaching looks like. To someone joining the profession, and starting to consider what constitutes effective teaching, there is probably an expectation that a universal consensus has emerged, resulting in several key principles underpinning the teaching tablets of stone. Whilst differences in emphasis do exist between educationalists, the three measures of effective teaching provided by Hay McBer (2000) offer the clearest guide to effective practice.

◆ Professional characteristics

Hay McBer argues that the way that the teacher goes about his job, the image he presents to his pupils, the manner in which he approaches difficult situations, and his overriding set of values have a significant impact on his ability to be an effective practitioner. His research points to strengths in five areas being required of all excellent teachers:

- professionalism (respect for others, confident, supportive and challenging, creates trust);
- thinking (analytical thinking, explaining cause and effect, and conceptual thinking, being able to identify themes over a period of time);
- planning and setting expectations (constant desire to see pupils develop, researching pupil strengths and weaknesses, demonstrating initiative to remediate quickly);
- relating to others (ability to empathize, being able to influence others, teamwork);
- leading (driving pupils towards their and teacher objectives, passion for learning, holding pupils to account, and flexibility).

This emphasis on teacher values and aims has had an impact on other studies, whilst failing to have a significant bearing on either Ofsted or the National Curriculum.

Hay McBer's findings were supported in an independent profile of 15 award-winning teachers by TES (2009). Using techniques usually deployed in business psychology, the study analysed their personalities, motivations and behaviour to identify seven habits that make them effective classroom practitioners. The seven habits they displayed were that they:

- build confidence amongst their students;
- are not afraid to make difficult decisions;
- develop others (students and colleagues);
- are good communicators;
- are non-conformists;
- thrive in the company of others;
- see the bigger picture.

Each of these fit neatly into Hay McBer's typology of professional characteristics, as they describe deep-seated patterns of behaviour that inform teachers' approach to the different situations which they are likely to face in a classroom on a daily basis.

◆ Teaching skills

In a meta-analysis of over 500,000 studies on 'what works' in the classroom, Professor John Hattie (2008) of Auckland University identified the following strategies as having the biggest effect on pupil performance:

- whole-class interactive (restricting the amount of teacher talk, with a variety of active tasks, such as graphic organizers, role-play, pair discussion, and regular feedback);
- feedback (delivered by the teacher during a lesson, with an emphasis on formative methods, and constructive comments on more formally assessed work – it can also be delivered effectively through peer evaluation);
- high expectations (setting challenging, but achievable tasks).

Teaching skills and professional characteristics are closely linked. Hay McBer argues that whilst skills can be learned, characteristics are more deeply embedded in an individual, and inform the approaches adopted by a particular teacher. So, if a teacher placed a great emphasis on individual responsibility, his teaching style might feature an emphasis on pupil self-evaluation, with pupils taking greater responsibility for their learning

◆ *Classroom climate*

The features of an effective learning environment are a key factor in creating a desire to learn. Hay McBer outlines nine 'dimensions' which are essential components of an effective learning environment (see Figure 1.1).

Why is it important to plan?

Implicit in the typology of an effective teacher is the requirement to plan. Whether the teacher is attempting to challenge pupil misconceptions, create exciting lessons, or establish a purposeful learning environment, it is impossible to have a positive impact on pupil progress without prior consideration of both objectives and approaches. It is tempting for less experienced colleagues to look at their battle-hardened colleagues' apparently casual approach to curriculum implementation and lesson preparation, and attempt to ape it. However, this temptation needs to be strongly resisted. Whilst it is good practice to review your teaching no matter what stage you are in your career, experienced teachers are more likely to have a clearer idea of the resources available and the learning needs of their pupils, and to have developed better time management skills allowing them to give the appearance of preparing a lesson 'off the cuff'.

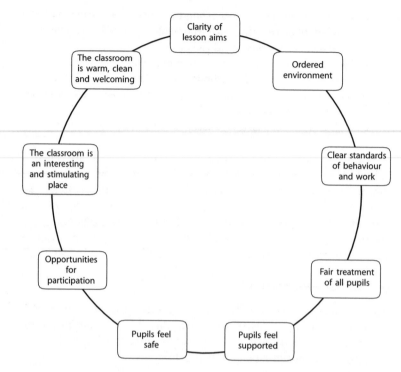

Figure 1.1 The dimensions of an effective learning environment (Hay McBer, 2000)

Haydn et al. (2001) provide a more refined explanation, and suggest four principal reasons why it is important to plan:

◆ *Keeping to your primary objective*

Faced with the many pressures of being a trainee or newly qualified teacher (NQT), it might be easy for a history teacher to lose sight of the primary objective: teaching about the past. Starting to teach history brings with it so many demands – a need to absorb curriculum structure, learn new periods of history, and possibly different types of post-14 and post-16 assessment, on top of every new teacher's inevitable concern over behaviour management – that an initial goal of teaching sequences of stimulating lessons is reduced to a sequence of unconnected exercises in filling a period. The consequences of such an approach are not only related to pupil underperformance; the teacher is likely to place himself under even greater stress if he is constantly stumbling from one lesson to another, which could well lead to additional problems with behaviour in the classroom and potentially, with the head of department.

◆ Covering all the ground

Placing greater emphasis on planning may help inexperienced and experienced teachers overemphasizing historical content in a lesson. Whilst meaningful exploration of the key processes needs to be placed in an appropriate historical context, if they are to have any academic value at all, there is a very real danger of the narrative dominating a lesson, if planning is not carefully thought through. History teachers need to take a medium- and long-term perspective to ensure that all the concepts and processes are covered throughout the year, and that there is an opportunity to develop these skills and processes across the key stage.

◆ Personalized learning and differentiation

Linking back to the qualities of an effective teacher, unprepared lessons frequently take a more directed instructional or didactic form than ones where attention to the pupils' precise learning needs has been paid. Good medium-term plans should have the flexibility to be amended in the light of new information. So, where it becomes clear that pupils are struggling with particular concepts, the scheme of work can be refined to meet their particular needs.

◆ It's a statutory requirement

Finally, placed in the context of a teacher training or induction programme, longer-and short-term planning is a statutory requirement. The standards required to gain Qualified Teacher Status include:

Q10 Have a knowledge and understanding of a range of teaching, learning and behaviour management strategies and know how to use and adapt them, including how to personalise learning and provide opportunities for all learners to achieve their potential.

Q13 Know how to use local and national statistical information to evaluate the effectiveness of their teaching, to monitor the progress of those they teach and to raise levels of attainment.

Q15 Know and understand relevant statutory and non-statutory curricula, frameworks, including those provided through the National Strategies, for their subjects/curriculum areas, and other relevant initiatives applicable to the age and ability range for which they are trained.

Q22 Plan for progression across the age and ability range for which they are trained, designing effective learning sequences within lessons and across series of lessons and demonstrating secure subject/curriculum knowledge.

Q23 Design opportunities for learners to develop their literacy, numeracy and ICT skills.

Q24 Plan homework or other out-of-class work to sustain learners' progress and to extend and consolidate their learning.

Q25 Teach lessons and sequences of lessons across the age and ability range for which they are trained in which they: (a) use a range of teaching strategies and resources, including e-learning, taking practical account of diversity and promoting equality and inclusion; (b) build on prior knowledge, develop concepts and processes, enable learners to apply new knowledge, understanding and skills and meet learning objectives; ... (d) manage the learning of individuals, groups and whole classes, modifying their teaching to suit the stage of the lesson.

Q26 (b) Assess the learning needs of those they teach in order to set challenging learning objectives.

Q29 Evaluate the impact of their teaching on the progress of all learners, and modify their planning and classroom practice where necessary.

Once qualified, there is still a formal requirement to demonstrate proficiency in planning. In order to obtain Newly Qualified Teacher Status, to move beyond Threshold, and even achieve Excellent teacher status, planning is one of the key areas assessed (see Table 1.1, p. 11).

How can I improve my long- and medium-term planning?

Long-term planning usually refers to the approach taken to cover an entire key stage. Without careful thought about how the different units fit together, there is a real danger of creating a KS3 curriculum that lacks cohesion, fails to develop the key historical skills, and impedes the development of secure chronological understanding.

Table 1.1 Planning skills required for Newly Qualified Teacher Status

Core	Post-threshold	Excellent
C26 Plan for progression across the age and ability range they teach, designing effective learning sequences within lessons and across series of lessons informed by secure subject/curriculum knowledge	P7 Be flexible, creative and adept at designing learning sequences within lessons and across lessons that are effective and consistently well-matched to learning objectives and the needs of learners, and which integrate recent developments, including those relating to subject/ curriculum knowledge.	E7 (a) Take a lead in planning collaboratively with colleagues in order to promote effective practice. (b) Identify and explore links within and between subjects/curriculum areas in their planning.
C27 Design opportunities for learners to develop their literacy, numeracy, ICT and thinking and learning skills appropriate within their phase and context.		
C28 Plan, set and assess homework, other out-of-class assignments and coursework for examinations, where appropriate, to sustain learners' progress and to extend and consolidate their learning		

Source: http://www.tda.gov.uk/teachers/professionalstandards/standards/skills/planning/core.aspx

QCDA's Innovating with History website (http://curriculum. qcda.gov.uk/key-stages-3-and-4/subjects/key-stage-3/ history/index.aspx) provides a long list of features which ought to guide long-term planning, but I have outlined what I regard as the ten most important below:

1. Maintain historical enquiry at the heart of the units.
2. Ensure that all the major themes, events and regions are included.
3. Include a variety of resources.
4. Make provision for use of ICT to enhance opportunities for the effective teaching of history.

5. Consider history's role in the curriculum: what cross-curricular links are included?
6. Identify areas where history's link to citizenship can be explored.
7. Use an appropriate blend of overview and depth, ensuring overview knowledge supports depth and vice versa.
8. Provide a means to ensure historical knowledge, skills and understanding are built up in an organized, systematic and rigorous way based on learning that has already taken place.
9. Include a range of approaches to teaching and learning including experiences outside the classroom.
10. Inspire pupils and motivate them to continue studying history.

In practice, there are several issues a department needs to consider when constructing a new scheme of work for history at KS3. These include:

- the time available for the subject, including homework;
- how to ensure continuity from KS2;
- how to ensure coherence and progression in knowledge, skills and understanding across the key stage;
- what time to allocate to each of the six studies (Britain 1066–1500, Britain 1500–1750, Britain 1750–1900, a European study before 1914, a world study before 1900, a world study after 1900) in order to achieve breadth and balance across KS3;
- whether to structure the long-term plan in a broadly chronological framework or whether to use the flexibility of the revised programme of study to devise a different framework;
- how to plan an appropriate blend of overview and depth, ensuring that overview knowledge supports depth and vice versa;
- the implications of decisions for resources;
- use activities and resources, including ICT, that involve pupils and enable them to take increasing responsibility

In theory, one of the biggest challenges is ensuring the right blend of overview and depth, so that pupils gain a suitably detailed insight into a period, whilst being able to place it into a broader historical, or geographical context. Several factors conspire to make this task more difficult, including the limited curriculum time devoted to history, and the extremely broad scope of the National Curriculum. There is a danger inherent in the diverse units within the National Curriculum of providing a series of fascinating isolated enquires, but failing to provide the necessary linkage to create a coherent overview of a period.

Work done by Michael Riley, Director of the Schools History Project has informed much of what has been written on this topic. He attempted to reconcile the need for depth and breadth through the development of his 'big stories and big pictures' approach (Riley, 1997). This involved teachers incorporating overviews into their schemes of work, to accompany depth studies. This could involve providing a broader European context, for example when looking at changes in religion under the Tudors, or moving beyond well-trodden political effects to examine social or economic circumstances at the time. In this case, a study of the feudal system could support an enquiry into kingship during the Middle Ages.

According to Riley, the chief advantages of using overviews are that they provide support for lower-achieving pupils, allowing them to see how 'smaller stories' can fit into bigger ones, whilst providing opportunities for more able pupils to make links to other aspects of the period.

Riley's ideas have been developed in a series of articles in *Teaching History*, but his basic model offers a practical and effective way to deliver historical overviews, whilst teaching a depth study. Strategies for implementing this approach could include the following:

- Teaching the overview first in order to set the scene or to stimulate interest in the depth study to come. By framing the overview as a hypothesis, the pupils could attempt to tackle the issue through smaller in-depth enquiries, and assess the validity of the original hypothesis in an end-of-unit assessment. One method for engaging pupils' interest in a hypothesis is to use a range of source material which is clearly supportive of a particular viewpoint. When I teach the First World War to Year 9 pupils, I focus on the popular view of the war as being all about mud, machine guns and misery. By assembling a sequence of video clips, photographs and war poems into a short film, using Microsoft Movie Maker, I ask the pupils to note down what impression of the war they get from the different images. They then email me their thoughts, and I input them all into a Wordle document. This amazing web-based software (http://www.wordle.net) reshapes a body of text into graphical forms, highlighting commonly used words or phrases. The benefit of using Wordle for the overview is that it will emphasize the key elements of the hypothesis. In this case, words such as 'slaughter', 'rain', 'mud', 'trenches', 'death' *should* dominate, providing us with a clear focus for our enquiries about the war.

- Building up multiple thematic overviews across several depth studies. Pupils could be referred to the different themes throughout the depth studies, and a synoptic task could take an overall view of the different themes. For example, a series of units exploring the origins and features of revolutions could also compare the role of common factors, such as individuals or economic problems.
- Different groups focusing on separate depth studies, as part of an exploration of a bigger overall enquiry. Through presentations to the rest of the class, or structured group work, they work together to construct the overview. This approach can also be used to construct an initial overview, as outlined in the first bullet point. When I introduce new topics at A level, I sometimes ask pupils to compile a glossary of the major figures or concepts which they will encounter during their study. After each pupil has completed their short task, they have to peer-review each other's work. As this is usually tackled on the school's Virtual Learning Environment, it is relatively straightforward to edit each other's work.
- Outlining the context in which an event takes place. The 'Meet the King' lesson outlined below as an example of short-term planning provides one example of how this approach could be used to support Year 8 pupils in their introduction to Henry VIII and his break with Rome.

As teachers move from long-term to medium-term planning, they need to pay greater attention to prior learning, the role of the enquiry within the long-term plan (and overview), the expectations of pupil performance on that unit, and specific resources required to create inspiring and challenging lessons, and support out-of-class activities. It will also be necessary to outline the focus of each lesson within the unit.

Figures 1.2 and 1.3 are templates for constructing both the overview and depth elements of a medium-term plan, and comments are provided for guidance.

Main enquiry	It is important to frame this as an open question, allowing the opportunity for argument and study of interpretations
Overview of the unit	A brief summary of what the unit will focus on, key concepts and processes to be considered, and length of time allocated to its study.
Rationale for the unit	Identify where the enquiry fits into the Programme of Study, as well as the broader historical, conceptual or geographical context. Any links to cross-curricular themes or citizenship should also be highlighted.
Expectations of pupil progress	Typically, a plan of this kind will include a variation on the following format: At the end of this unit, most pupils will be able to: Some pupils will be able to: Some pupils will have progressed further, and will be able to:
Assessment strategies	How will you monitor progression through the enquiry?
Prior learning	Link to previous units, learning approaches, processes, concepts or vocabulary
Important vocabulary	If specialized words or phrases are likely to impede the understanding of the content feature, draw up a list in advance
Resources	List textbooks, video clips, websites. It can save time later on, if these are classified under different headings, related to sections of the unit

Figure 1.2 Constructing the overview of a medium-term plan

Key questions	National Curriculum concepts/ processes	Lesson focus	Learning outcomes	Suggested resources	Out-of-class activity
These are the mini-enquiries used to answer the overarching unit enquiry.	Refer specifically to the National Curriculum, eg. chronology/critical reflection Give careful thought to how you can cover most of the key concepts (chronological understanding, cultural, ethnic and religious diversity, change and continuity, cause and consequence) and processes (historical enquiry, using evidence, communicating about the past) within the enquiry.

Within the broader context of the KS3 plan, you will have to demonstrate how you will map pupil progression across each of the concepts and processes. | Outline the starter/ main tasks/plenary of each lesson This is the stage in the planning process where you will need to take into account the different clearing needs of your pupils. Have you tried to use a variety of teaching strategies to support different learning styles or specific educational needs? | How pupil understanding is likely to be assessed, e.g. through posters, role-play, mini whiteboards, written responses | Refer to textbooks, websites, worksheets, timelines etc. It might be a good idea to identify which resources likely to be used have not yet been created. This will act as a prompt and, hopefully, prevent last minute scurrying around! | You may include possible homework tasks, perhaps crossing different key questions. Links to accompanying websites, or likely field trip possibilities could also figure here |

Figure 1.3 Constructing a medium-term plan in depth

What should my lesson plans look like?

Successive Ofsted reports have outlined what an effective lesson plan should look like. The 2001/02 subject report for history praised one lesson where 'carefully crafted lesson structure which ensured that they understood what was required of them' (Ofsted, 2002), and the 2007 report *History in the Balance* (Ofsted, 2007) identified, amongst other features, the main criteria for a successful lesson plan:

- use effective teaching methods that encourage pupils to take responsibility, capture pupils' imagination and engage them;
- make effective use of support staff who themselves fully understand the purposes of the work;
- use activities and resources, including ICT, that involve pupils and enable them to take increasing responsibility;
- question skilfully and effectively to assess pupils' progress and extend their thinking and understanding;
- enable discussion and debate amongst pupils;
- assess pupils' work effectively and systematically and use the information to plan to meet individuals' needs.

The Assessment Reform Group (1999) provides a detailed summary of how effective planning needs to involve several assessment strategies. These include sharing learning goals with pupils, helping pupils to know and to recognize the standards they are aiming for, involving pupils in self-assessment, and providing feedback which leads to pupils recognizing their next steps and how to take them.

In a profile of 'what History teachers do in the classroom', Husbands *et al.*'s (2003) observations of real classroom activity supported Ofsted's findings on key characteristics of successful short-term lesson planning. The dominant feature of the lessons which they observed was the use of effective questioning by the teacher. Effective questioning is one of the core teaching skills outlined earlier in the chapter, and is an important tool for moving pupils on, assessing understanding, challenging preconceptions, and providing a focus for the lesson as a whole. Effective teachers try to use a range of questioning techniques:

- challenging questions which require higher-order thinking such as analysis, evaluation or synthesis;
- clearly expressed, open-ended questions which allow a range of responses and provide an opportunity for the teacher to gradually hone in on more precise issues;
- changing the wording of the question to assess different levels of understanding;
- changing the focus of the question – whole class, individual pupils, pairs.

A further feature of the lessons which they observed was a mix of independent activity and teacher-led instruction. Hattie is very clear in stressing the importance of whole-class interactive approaches, where pupils are set tasks or problems, but with clear guidance and structure from the teacher. Examples of this type of independent activity could include, for example:

- graphic organizers, such as comparison tables or flow diagrams;
- think, pair, share activities;
- role-play;
- card sorts;
- source evaluation;
- living graphs.

Finally, the importance of stressing and sharing the learning goals was found to be critical. These goals either took the form of concepts or processes to be developed, usually linked to content-driven outcomes, or also incorporated broader educational objectives, such as literacy, numeracy, or citizenship. It is tempting for trainee teachers and NQTs to cram a large number of objectives into a single lesson. After all, don't we all want to make greatest use of the time available to us in a lesson? However, you have to consider how much is achievable in a single lesson, and, more importantly, how much the pupils are likely to remember when they leave the classroom, or even a few hours later. There is an apocryphal tale of a football manager trying to demonstrate the futility of giving complex team talks immediately prior to a match. To do so, he gave every player a 'key fact' to remember, and, at half time, he asked each of them what their 'key fact' was. The failure of most of the players to remember their fact seemed to prove his point. Now the strategies deployed in a classroom to enhance the quality of learning will be far more productive than simply issuing a mere

detail, but the basic argument is valid: it is important to focus on what is achievable and likely to make an impact. It is therefore perfectly acceptable to focus on a single objective, and certainly do not attempt to achieve more than three.

Most teachers will include the outlining of lesson objectives, or learning outcomes, in their starter activity, usually by linking that lesson's work back to work covered in previous lessons. This is good practice, as pupils travelling to history from French or maths frequently need reminding about the last thing they covered in history, and they will need reintroducing to the key enquiry they are working towards.

The danger in this approach, however, is that starters become formulaic, and pupils disengage even before you have finished sharing the objectives with them. How you start your lesson probably requires more thought than any other aspect; if the pupils are not inspired to work, or do not know what they are working towards, then all your hard work preparing tasks for the remainder of the lesson will come to nought. The 'Meet the King' lesson outlined in Figure 1.4 uses the announcement of a special guest and a quick change into royal clothing to get the pupils' attention, but you do not have to don different outfits to engage their attention. Other methods could include the following:

- Recall tennis. Ask the pupils to draw a straight line down a scrap of paper. This is the 'court', with the line representing a 'net'. In pairs, pupils have to alternately provide three points each from the previous lesson, writing on either side of the 'net'. The first pair to write down six points between them win. Pupils, especially boys, love a competitive element in a lesson, and this task provides a quick link to previous work.
- Video clip. This can work well if you do not provide any introduction. The pupils could then be asked questions about the clip, in order to try to guess its significance. If you are technologically capable enough, you could previously edit the clip to replace the dialogue from the clip with your own soundtrack. You could then ask the pupils what they thought was taking place, or what the people in the clip were saying or thinking. Most history departments enjoy a good range of documentary-style videos/DVDs and history-based movies. Using a clip from Oliver Stone's *Platoon* could be a good introduction into the reasons for the USA's withdrawal from Vietnam, whilst YouTube and Google Video will provide a fertile hunting ground for teachers eager to acquire a more esoteric collection of video clips.

- Play music/video as the pupils enter the lesson. One of my most effective starters is used to begin a GCSE unit on Nazi Germany. As the pupils enter the classroom, a clip from Leni Riefenstahl's documentary about the 1936 Berlin Olympics plays on the whiteboard (this can be downloaded at http://www.youtube.com/watch?v=MRttjfprkXU&feature=related). I use a section at the start when the classical figures become alive, and the Olympic torch travels across a map of Europe from Greece to Germany. It is a great way to settle the pupils, get them curious about the topic, and to subsequently discuss the messages being transmitted in the clip. From this point we can ask what type of regime would want to present itself in this way, and how could they come to power. Straight into the Weimar Republic we go...

Playing music can be a good way to help pupils really get a feel for the topic they are studying. Even my Year 13 pupils are not immune to the effects of the Platoon soundtrack as they enter a lesson exploring the failure of the US ground war in South East Asia!

- Art. I often use art as a way into a new topic. Before the pupils enter the classroom, I distribute a picture from the period which they are about to study, and a small piece of scrap paper. Once they are settled, I ask them to draw a small face on the paper. After they have done this, I tell them to carefully rip out the face from the paper, and place it on any character in the picture. From this point, I tell them, they are that character. I then question them on what they can see, hear, smell, feel. All of this is done to give them a (superficial) feel for the period, and it often provides a fun way in tot the topic. Pupils use it as an opportunity to make comparisons between the society portrayed in the picture with modern-day living. More able pupils could also be asked to comment on the usefulness of the source to a historian studying that period. In this way, they begin to evaluate its strengths and weaknesses.
- Puppets. I once read an article which suggested using puppets to represent historical characters in a retelling of an event. This sounds like a great idea, but I have not yet summoned up the courage to either risk the wrath of my daughters for taking their princess puppets into school, or the likelihood of humiliation in front of my hard-nosed Year 8s as I outline the story of Elizabeth and Mary, Queen of Scots!

The examples above represent but a small range of possible starters. In the context of the lesson, the starter is merely the hook to get the class interested. The skilful teacher then has to manage the transition between the starter and the first task, the first task and the second task, and the second task and the plenary. Throughout the lesson, the pupils need to know where they are going and the purpose of the route which they are being taken along. Regular reference to, and informal assessment of, the lesson objectives is a useful way to achieve this.

Trying to incorporate all of these features into a single lesson plan is a daunting task for many teachers, but especially for those starting in the profession. Whilst the development of a medium-term scheme of work will have mapped out a macro-approach, the teacher has to consider how to turn the stated aims of the longer enquiry into a single lesson. The example in Figure 1.4 suggests how this can be achieved.

Tasks

1. Try to develop engaging starters for lessons on the following topics:
   - The causes of the Wall Street Crash
   - The social effects of the Industrial Revolution
   - The Treaty of Versailles
   - The reputation of King John
   - Henry VIII and the English Reformation
2. Review the section on Michael Riley's use of overviews. Consider different ways in which you can incorporate a 'big picture' into your existing KS3 curriculum, and one of the key enquiries within it. Try to use different ways of providing an overview. Will you use the chronological context, or perhaps a more specific theme, such as the role of individuals? In the light of your work, reflect on how the schemes of work might have to be amended in order to teach the overview more effectively.

Name: Neil Smith

Class: 8P

Number of pupils: 27

Number of pupils with SEN: 3

Length of Lesson: 40 minutes

Main enquiry: Why did Henry VIII create his own Church?

Previous learning: England in 1500

Lesson objectives:

Pupils will be able to provide an overview of what the young Henry VIII was like.
Pupils will develop ICT presentation skills to communicate about the past.
Pupils will develop chronological understanding of early Tudor England.

Content, processes and concepts addressed

	Pupil activity	Teacher activity	Resources	Time:
Starter	Listen	Explain that a special guest is due to visit the class today, who is going to help us understand what young Henry was like...hide behind desk, don gown and plastic crown Seamlessly transform into the young Henry VIII	'Meet the King' handout, outlining the pupil activities for the first task Use computer to play 'Greensleeves' whilst 'transforming' into Henry	5 minutes
Task 1:	In the role of newspaper reporters at a special royal press conference, they question Henry about his personality, interests, family, aspirations, attitudes towards kingship. Note down responses provided by the king. The responses will inform their homework	Respond to questions Prompt group, when they seem to be running out of ideas	Effective questioning to move them on – does not provide the answers, forces the pupils to think	15 minutes
Task 2: Peer assessment – AfL in action!	Through pair question and answer, pupils share their observations on the young king	Remove royal garb and return to teacher mode		10 minutes

	Pupil activity	Teacher activity	Resources	Time:
Plenary	Pupils use mini whiteboards to identify most important characteristic of Henry's personality	Whole class review of the main points about young Henry. (link back to lesson objectives). Discuss what people might want to know about Henry, and whether we can trust what he said in the press conference	Whiteboard to reinforce key points	10 minutes
Homework	Write a newspaper article about the new king		Worksheet on how to produce a newspaper in Microsoft Word	
Provision for SEN (indicate type, e.g. dyslexia, G&T)	Provide sheet with main points about Henry VIII at the end of the lesson. Variety of task. Forcing pupils to come up with the questions, and allowing them to decide which features about Henry to write about, provides challenge for more able pupils			

Review of whole class understanding

Figure 1.4 Constructing a lesson plan to meet the needs of longer term enquiries

Carrying out meaningful assessment

2

This chapter aims to equip teachers with the necessary tools to assess their pupils' understanding of history in an effective manner. It combines a mixture of theory, recent educational advice, and tried and tested methods to outline an extensive array of useful strategies.

What is assessment and why is it so important?

In simple terms, assessment is concerned with gauging how much an individual knows or understands about a particular topic or unit of study. However, within this very general description, one can distinguish between two forms of assessment which, whilst superficially exclusive, can be mutually supporting.

Most traditional concepts of assessment are based on formal tests designed to provide a final judgement on performance, usually for an external audience such as parents, examination boards, universities, employers, and government departments. These are known as *summative* assessments. Examples of these include end of key stage level descriptor-based assessments, GCSEs, A levels, the IB and Pre-U. In short, written summative assessments provide the most widely used method of determining a pupil's competence in history at key transition points.

The other form of assessment provides a more fluid link between teaching and learning and assessment. *Formative* assessment aims to inform both teacher and pupil about the quality of learning, and the ways in which the subject is being delivered on a more frequent basis than traditional summative means, and in a more informal manner. Whilst summative assessment could be described as assessment *of* learning, formative assessment is commonly labelled as Assessment *for* Learning (AfL) as it seeks to involve the pupil to a much greater extent in evaluating their own progress, and requires the teacher to adopt a more flexible approach to amending their teaching in the light of their assessment of pupils' progress within and between lessons. The information provided to pupils in formative assessment tends to be more varied too. With a greater focus on helping to improve, greater emphasis is placed on comments rather than grades or marks, acknowledging the importance of raising self-esteem amongst pupils and presenting them with information which they can understand and act upon.

Of course, the two forms of assessment are not quite as exclusive as the two descriptions above might suggest. In practice, all teachers use end-of-module tests to inform their planning and priorities for teaching subsequent topics, whilst effective reviews of tests in class enable pupils to identify their own areas for development.

Why, then, has so much attention been directed towards forms of assessment in recent years? Why is it so important?

◆ Assessment raises standards

Successive Ofsted reports (for example, Ofsted 1998, Section 5.6) testify to the main role of assessment in the curriculum: to raise standards. By providing a means to track pupil progress and to make diagnostic judgements on their strengths and weaknesses, assessment is a key tool in improving the quality of learning and teaching. A meta-study of existing assessment and learning undertaken by Black and Wiliam (1998b) found that implementing formative strategies could result in an increase of up to two grades at GCSE for individual pupils (Assessment Reform Group, 1999).

For teachers, assessment provides an effective means to evaluate their own teaching. Whether using formative or summative methods, it allows them to evaluate whether the material is sufficiently challenging for the more able pupils and to identify which pupils need further support. It also enables them to identify which areas or skills need further attention. Careful analysis of data from GCSE or A-level modules will identify areas for future attention, such as source skills or knowledge and understanding.

◆ *Personalized learning*

Related to the previous point, assessment is a crucial feature of the personalized learning agenda. It is probably the most informative and accurate tool for giving information in individual pupil performance, and thus enables the teacher to set targets for pupils, rather than classes. The research by Black and Wiliam referred to above suggests that meaningful assessment can improve grades. The introduction of the Assessing Pupil Progress (APP) strategy attempts to put these ideas into the practice, with its intention to help teachers *fine-tune their understanding of pupils' needs and tailor their planning and teaching accordingly.*

◆ *Learning to learn*

A further way in which assessment contributes to the personalization agenda is by helping pupils learn how to learn. Receiving any kind of feedback on progress can assist pupils decide which learning strategies are most effective for them, such as visual, auditory or kinaesthetic, and force them to take greater responsibility for monitoring their own performance.

◆ *A motivational tool*

Assessment can also perform a critical role in motivating pupils to both succeed and perform badly. When pupils do well in assessments, or when feedback is positive and constructive, with clear suggestions for improvement, the confidence of the learner and their motivation to succeed will develop. Where feedback is overly critical, or focuses primarily on grading, it will not be too long before a pupil becomes demoralized and therefore at greater risk of failure.

◆ *What and how to learn*

Pupils can also gain a greater insight into what is important to learn, as well as how to learn from various forms of assessment. In the same way that teachers benefit from analysing which aspects of a course require further attention, so too can pupils appreciate whether areas such as content or skills need to be focused on. This is something that pupils often find difficult, and they can struggle to identify areas of development in terms more specific than general references to 'sources' or 'essay writing'.

◆ *The external audience*

Formal examinations also provide useful data for an audience beyond the classroom. Subject leaders can compare how their students are performing in comparison to other subjects, and in comparison to previous cohorts. Recent statistical innovations such as Edexcel's 'Resultsplus' have placed a huge amount of information at the fingertips of heads of department, and facilitate quite detailed analysis of examination results.

In an age where league tables are the primary reference point for comparing different schools, assessments can allow parents, local authorities and central government to make judgements about the performances of different schools. In this way, they perform a (sometimes contested) evaluative function, as outside agencies use them to make their evaluation of the success or otherwise of a particular school.

What are the features of good assessment?

In order for assessment to be most effective, it has to be performed effectively. Failure to do so could result in the accumulation of useless information about the performance of pupils and teachers, and seriously undermine the confidence of learners. Scott-Baumann et al. (1997), Phillips (2002) and, more recently, Ofsted (2003) have outlined the main criteria of effective assessment. Some suggestions are provided in Figure 2.1.

◆ *Assessment for Learning and history*

The key texts for any teacher wanting to understand the development of the AfL agenda are those authored by Paul Black and Dylan Wiliam: *Inside the Black Box* (1998a) and *Working Inside the Black Box* (2002). Their study of over 250 research papers and development of practice-based research have proven to be hugely influential in changing the way in which teachers view and use assessment.

AfL is chiefly concerned with bridging the gap between testing and teaching, and aims to incorporate greater assessment of pupil understanding within lessons, as opposed to relying on conventional summative forms of assessment. A further difference is

Clear objectives	Informs, but does not dictate planning	Variety of forms	Feedback is meaningful	Consistency and reliability	Part of the teaching process
• Do the pupils know why they are being assessed? • Are they aware of the assessment criteria? • Are the goals realistic and achievable?	• Are you able to amend your teaching in the light of assessment evidence?	• Do you make provision for different learning styles when assessing pupils?	• Do you provide a written comment? • Do you identify what has been done well … • And how the work can be improved?	• Do you use mark schemes to work? • Are they based on NCLevel Descriptors and/or departmental marking policy? • Do you use multiple assessments to make your judgement?	• Do you regularly assess understanding during the course of a lesson? • Are formal tests seen as part of a normal teaching unit?

Figure 2.1 Features of effective assessment

that AfL should be seen as a process, rather than an event or procedure. The ultimate goal is for pupils to become more independent in their approach, developing strategies for assessing their own practice, which, in turn, should make them more effective learners.

The four key principles underpinning AfL are as follows:

1. Pupils will learn more if they understand the purpose of their learning.
2. Pupil peer and self-assessment is a critical tool for improving performance. Pupils will learn more if they are aware of their own progress towards the stated objectives.
3. Pupils will learn more if they know how to close the gap between their present achievements and the desired learning goals.
4. Teachers will be more effective if they adopt formative methods of assessment (i.e. future teaching takes into account prior pupil performance). They can thus identify common errors made by the pupils, and any difficulties which they may be having with the work.

Assessment therefore becomes an ongoing process, and a central part of the teaching within a lesson. Necessarily it also becomes less formal, appearing organically in the same way that a starter, discussion, main task and plenary would. Figure 2.2 provides an example of how a typical lesson might operate, integrating a range of AfL strategies.

Providing opportunities for peer assessment and class discussion are useful ways to gauge levels of understanding throughout the class. However, for class discussion to work most effectively, teachers have to give considerable thought to the type of questions they ask. The purpose of these discussions is not simply to monitor the grasp of key facts, but to assess a deeper understanding of the material, and to prompt pupils to reflect on their own thought processes themselves. Black and Wiliam (2002) give examples of questioning techniques provided by teachers who participated in their practice-based research project. These included the following:

- Not allowing pupils to put their hand up after a question has been asked. Everyone is expected to be able to contribute, so that the discussion does not revolve around a small number of people in the class. Online random name generators, such as that found at www.classtools.net, add an element of fun to the selection process!
- Allowing increased thinking time after asking the question.

Stage in lesson	Feature	Activity	Assessment purpose
Starter	1. Recap work from previous lesson on outbreak of WW1. 2. Share lesson objectives with the class: what the pupils should hope to achieve by the end of the lesson. These may also be written on the board, and the teacher may also differentiate expectations.	In pairs, pupils alternatively list six main reasons why the war started. Class discussion follows, where gaps in pupil knowledge are dealt with. Use stimulus material and teacher exposition. Teacher reminds group of assessment criteria, published on the classroom wall, and stuck into the exercise book.	Identify who does and does not understand the work from the previous lesson Teacher is sharing the criteria for success with every pupil
Activity	Pupils carry out task	Teacher discusses work with pupils. May choose to choose a 'traffic light' strategy…asks pupils to hold up a 'green' card if pupils are comfortably working towards the task's objectives, 'amber' if they are basically fine, but need a little clarification, or a 'red' one if they need help reaching the task's objectives. Where there are causes for concern, teacher discusses the issue and provides suggestions for further progress.	For the pupils who displayed green or amber cards, they remain engaged and on task, whilst those who held up red cards will gain and insight into how they can improve, and hopefully, become more confident in their ability to progress

Stage in lesson	Feature	Activity	Assessment purpose
Plenary	Assess progress towards learning objectives	Teacher reminds class of lesson objectives. In pairs, pupils assess each other's work. Teacher distributes a sheet with assessment criteria, and space for pupils to write 2 points for 'what was done well' and 2 points for 'how it could be improved'. Alternatively, the teacher could ask the pupils to identify their own criteria for success. A discussion of the different criteria could then inform the bulk of the class discussion at the end of the lesson. Pupils given time to reflect on their learning, with brief class discussion	Pupils encouraged to participate i n their own learning and that of their peers. Reminder of assessment criteria and lesson objectives.

Figure 2.2 Integrating AfL strategies into a lesson plan

- Although teachers might experience a little uneasiness at first, especially if there are no responses, every pupil is given the opportunity to consider a response, which in turn benefits the whole class, and should result in more developed responses being provided. Where there is access to learning response systems (or voting pods), the teacher can insist on a response from all pupils (most recent versions of these pods allow text input), and to establish a time frame which gives all pupils sufficient opportunity to consider their response.
- Greater attention to the type of question being asked. By moving away from closed recall questions, and towards broader, enquiry-based questioning, the discussion relates more closely to the objective of the lesson, and forces the pupils to think beyond a simple, singular response. It will also encourage more participation if there is no single answer to the question.
- Prompting pupils to explain the reasoning behind their response helps the teacher make an assessment of the depth of understanding, and to provide an additional challenge to able pupils.
- All of the above are essential to the creation of a supportive learning environment. This is necessary to give all pupils confidence in their ability to contribute, sustain their motivation to succeed, and maintain their enjoyment in the subject. This can further be enhanced when pupils actually have the confidence to get things wrong, knowing that they will not get instantly corrected or admonished. This might require the teacher to refine their own approach, to the point where they become more concerned with drawing out ideas from the whole class rather than getting the correct answer to a series of quick fire questions.
- Feedback should not be driven by the need to match pupil responses to the Level Descriptors. Not only will this turn the discussion into a mechanical process where the ebb and flow of historical debate is reduced to a checklist of targets and standards, but it will also potentially dent pupil aspiration. As the editorial in *Teaching History* 131 (Counsell et al., 2008) explains very clearly, history is not about moving sequentially and consistency up a ladder of progression. Pupils develop some skills before others, and progress in some areas more rapidly than others. In this way, overemphasis on levelling throughout every lesson could actually undermine the very benefits AfL is designed to create.

Some practical examples of how formative assessment can be carried out using the formats of old television shows is provided in Figure 2.3. This is taken directly from my web-based collection of teaching ideas 'What Went Well?', which can be found at http://whatwentwell.blogspot.com/ (you need to have a Google account or be signed up to blogger.com to view it).

70s throwback

Recreating lost classics of 70s TV is a neat way to use mini whiteboards, and assess understanding...

1. *Mr and Mrs*. Divide the group into pairs, each partner has to write down what the other one thinks is the answer to a particular question. Assuming that the class does not have telepathic powers, what you are trying to do is to elicit a range of reasons/results for discussion ... if the pair offer different responses, you can discuss which is the strongest reason/result.
2. *Blankety Blank*. Divide the class into 2 teams ... one member of each team comes to the front, and is asked a question. Every member of the team has to write down what they think is the correct answer/explanation etc. The team member at the front has to select someone from his team to provide an answer ... a point is awarded if the two answers match.
3. *Family Fortunes*. The teacher has a range of possible responses to a broad question (e.g. why did the USA go to war in Korea?), arranged in hierarchy of importance, on a PowerPoint slide. The class is divided into teams of 4 ... each team has to discuss which response to write on their whiteboard ... they have to consider which is likely to be the highest ranked response on the slide. Teams get a point if their answer is in the list, and a further point for the highest ranked response amongst the teams, and 5 points in total for getting the top answer.

Figure 2.3 Novel ways to use formative assessment

Of course, AfL principles should also underpin the approach to marking pieces of work produced by pupils. In the first instance, the features of assessment included in the lesson above will also be present when doing formal marking: pupils should be familiar with the purpose of the task; assessment criteria should be shared; when pupils are producing an extended piece or work, the teacher may decide to allow pupils to produce drafts, or perform a 'progress review' on their own or another pupil's work.

When the work is graded, the teacher should aim to be consistent with his own standard of marking for all pupils, and to also be as consistent as possible with the standards and methods of marking of his colleagues. In this respect, the development of a departmental marking policy is an essential strategy. Figure 2.4 provides a generic marking policy produced by the History Department in a high-achieving school in Manchester. A copy of this is displayed in each history classroom, and an A5 version is stuck into every pupil's exercise book.

As well as publishing its assessment criteria, this particular history department distributes advice on how to improve performance to every pupil (Figure 2.5).

At my school, the department also encourages pupils to take responsibility for their own progress in different ways. Pupils in KS3 and KS4 record their marks on a sheet in their books (like that in Figure 2.6). The purpose of doing this is to inculcate in pupils an instinctive desire to monitor their progress during the course of a year, so that they can see for themselves when they are not working to their full potential. This particular document could be easily amended to include individual targets, and written comments by the pupil on their progress at a regular interval.

MONITORING YOUR PROGRESS IN HISTORY

Years 7–9 (ages 11–14)

How will I be assessed?
Most pieces of work completed in class or for homework will be graded on a scale of 1–10, with 10 being the highest. A summative comment will also be provided, which will suggest ways in which you can make improvements to your work in future. *Typically*, your marks should be interpreted as follows:

9–10 (A) Outstanding in every way. Full answers are provided, providing very good range and depth. There may be evidence of further research. Consistent performance at this standard should result in an A grade on your Reports.

6–8 (B) Answers suggest a good understanding of the material, but all aspects of a question may not be fully appreciated. You may not have completed each part of the task. Consistent performance at this standard is likely to result in an B or C grade on your Reports.

1–5 (C) Work may be largely incomplete, contains serious errors, or shows signs of being rushed. You should expect to repeat any work which falls into this category. Consistent performance at this standard should result in a U on your Report.

Figure 2.4 Sample marking policy

How can I improve my performance or further develop my interest in history?

In the first instance, you should always speak to your history teacher. In most cases, pupils lose marks because they may:

- Fail to answer all parts of a task
- Fail to focus on the question set
- Fail to include sufficient detail
- Offer a narrow range of points when explaining the reasons for or results of an event
- Where evaluation of sources is required, answers may not consider fully consider the reliability or usefulness of a source. Own knowledge may not be integrated with the source, or the answer may be imbalanced.
- Spend insufficient time preparing their work

Avoid all of these and look forward to consistent outstanding achievement in history!

Figure 2.5 Sample advice on improving performance

How am I doing?

Plot your progress during the year by ticking the appropriate box each time you receive a mark.

Task	Nature of task e.g. source exercise, extended writing (include total possible marks, and your actual mark)	9–10	6–8	1–5	How could I improve my work?

Figure 2.6 Pupil self-assessment template

Earlier in the chapter, I mentioned that the two main forms of assessment, summative and formative, were not as exclusive and their definitions might suggest. One way in which this can be illustrated is by presenting how this same history department encourages Year 11 pupils to review their performance in GCSE 'mock' examinations (Figure 2.7). Whilst these formal, written

---

Evaluating your performance in the 'mocks'

Section A: How well did you do?

Paper 1 mark:

Paper 2 mark:

Overall %:   Grade:

Previous examination %:

Section B: Breakdown of your marks

Question-by question analysis: briefly analyse how each of your answers for Papers 1 and 2 could have been improved

Section C: Assessing your performance

1. Would you say that your result is
   a) what you expected to achieve
   b) a surprise
   c) what you wanted to achieve
   d) below your expectations
   e) above your expectations
2. If you circled d) for question 1, which of the following statements best explains your under-performance
   a) lack of understanding overall
   b) difficulty with Paper 1 content
   c) difficulty with Paper technique
   d) difficulty with Paper 2 content
   e) difficulty with Paper 2 technique
   f) lack of revision
3. Which areas of content do you feel most uncertain about?

   PAPER 1

   PAPER 2

Figure 2.7 Pupil self-assessment template for post examination review

examinations are set primarily to assess understanding of units completed thus far, they can also serve an invaluable formative role if the post-examination feedback is carried out appropriately.

In this case, the pupil would be required to reflect on their performance in comparison to the previous summative assessment, carried out at the end of Year 10, and to focus on the areas for development for each question. Finally, section C invites the pupil to summarize their performance on the paper, and to consider which skills or topics of content require further attention in the period leading up to the GCSE examination.

When pupils move up to the sixth form, the benefits of using formative methods arguably increase, as pupils become more aware of their strengths and weaknesses, and more incentivized by the prospect of achieving a place at university. It is good practice at the start of the course to provide both a copy of the syllabus or departmental scheme of work, and the mark scheme. At this level, mark schemes tend to progress through a series of skills which a student can be expected to demonstrate in their response. For a 'traditional' essay, therefore, a levelled mark scheme might include:

L1 Irrelevant or inaccurate material.
L2 Predominantly descriptive or assertive.
L3 Most of the response tries to answer the question. However, some narrative elements might also be present, or the range of argument may not be extensive.
L4 About 70% of the answer has a good analytical focus, there is good range and development and a targeted conclusion. Some awareness of different viewpoints.
L5 First-rate analysis, with impressive range and depth and a clear sense of a debate.

The role of self-evaluation and peer assessment is also extremely valuable at this level too (see Figure 2.8).

Implicit in Figures 2.3–2.6 is the need to assign a grade or mark to each piece of work. Whilst the relationship between Level Descriptors and pupil progression will explored in more detail in the next section, it is worth taking a moment here to discuss the concept of 'comment-based marking', i.e. assessing work without reference to numbers, letters, or levels.

Black and Wiliam (1998a) argue strongly for greater use of comment-based marking, pointing to the negative effect which

A LEVEL SELF-EVALUATION SHEET

Name _____

Essay title _____

Mark _____

1. What suggestions were made to improve your essays when you received your last piece of work? How far have you managed to incorporate these suggestions into this essay?

2. Look at the Mark Scheme. Do you understand why your answer has been given a particular Level **and** Mark?

3. Comment on how far your answer contained each of the qualities of a successful A-level answer. These can be identified as:
   - Each paragraph begins with your argument, is followed by a brief explanation, then relevant supporting detail, and finally relates back to the question
   - You focus on the stated factor for half the answer, before offering alternative explanations
   - The conclusion targets the question, and offers links and hierarchy

4. Summary

Briefly describe what the main strengths and weaknesses of your answer were. What will you need to do in order to improve your mark next time?

Figure 2.8 Essay self-evaluation template

providing a mark *and* a comment has on pupil performance. Where both are given, pupils tend to ignore the comment, and thus miss out on the advice on how to improve their work. Understandably, teachers may be reluctant to omit marks, particularly when there is pressure from senior managers to regularly submit data on individual pupils.

The argument for only writing a comment gets to the heart of AfL: it is focused on using assessment to raise performance, by empowering the pupil to take greater responsibility for their own progress. Removing the grade forces the pupil to pay more attention to the comment, and, hopefully, to incorporate the suggestions into their next piece of work. Some teachers may still want to grade tasks, but keep the mark for their own records, and with the introduction of APP in 2010 (see below), teachers may feel that they will have to level a large number of tasks in order to make their judgement on a pupil. Even so, for the majority of work which a pupil completes, the research suggests that a written comment is more meaningful than providing a mark or grade.

For the comment to have the desired effect, several features need to be in place:

- It needs to go beyond the type of reinforcing statement which may have accompanied marks in the past.
- It needs to identify strengths of the work, such as where the pupil has managed to meet particular assessment criteria.
- It also needs to provide practical advice on how the task could be improved. In order to maintain the confidence of the pupil, it is good practice to offer three positive comments, and one tip for improvement.
- Black and Wiliam (2002) suggest that the full benefit of comment-based marking can only be achieved when time is provided in the lesson to reflect on the comments on the last piece of work. Identifying whether pupils have taken on board the comments can be done in a variety of ways. If there is time, they could be asked to rewrite the piece, taking into account the suggested improvements. With an extended piece of writing, they could be asked to complete a self-evaluation sheet similar to Figure 2.8, which requires the student to go back to the comments before writing the next task.

AfL is at the centre of the government's plan to improve standards in schools. The Department for Children, Schools and Families (DCSF) laid out its assessment strategy in 2008, and proclaimed its belief that assessment or learning is *central to effective teaching and learning* (DCSF, 2008: 2). The document states that the department's aims for AfL are:

every child knows how they are doing, and understands what they need to do to improve and how to get there....;
every teacher is equipped to make well-founded judgements about pupils' attainment, understands the concepts and principles of progression, and knows how to use their assessment judgements to forward plan, particularly for pupils who are not fulfilling their potential;
every school has in place structured and systematic assessment systems

for making regular, useful, manageable and accurate assessments of
pupils, and for tracking their progress;
every parent and carer knows how their child is doing, what they need
to do to improve, and how they can support the child and their
teachers.

(DCSF, 2008: 4)

In order to achieve this, teachers are going to have give much
greater thought to short- and long-term planning. In the short
term, they will need to decide on a range of learning objectives
which need to be met, the activities which are best suited to
meeting them in a lesson, the range of assessment strategies
which will be deployed to evaluate progress towards these
objectives, and the recording of pupil achievement. This will, in
turn, inform the objectives for future lessons, and the planning
cycle will begin again.

In the longer term, departments will have to consider how the
key concepts and processes in the Programme of Study (PoS)
should be covered during the course of a key stage, and the
different forms the assessments will take.

◆ *Assessing progression*

One of the biggest challenges facing history teachers is measuring
progression in pupils' historical thinking without becoming fixed
to the Level Descriptors – a practice which would, as stated
above, severely damage any attempt to create a fluid, dynamic
learning environment, and most likely result in flawed assessments of the pupils' strengths and weaknesses. This final part of
the chapter examines different approaches to measuring progression, and concludes with a summary of APP: the three letters
certain to strike fear into every teacher during the course of
2010/11.

Once upon a time, assessment of history focused on first-order
(or substantive) concepts, which dwelt on terms such as
parliament, king, noble, and church. Underpinning this approach
was a belief that knowing more was the same as being better. The
main problem with this approach was that it was not distinctly
historical; all subjects require the accumulation of knowledge.

By 1991, with the advent of the National Curriculum for
History, a more sophisticated approach was introduced. Instead
of concentrating on the 'what' of history, the NC shifted the
focus to the 'how'. Second-order concepts, such as cause,

change, and empathy, which relate to the process of actually doing history, dominated the structure which was devised to assess historical understanding. Assessing pupil progression would now be based on understanding the ways that history was done, rather than measuring how much someone knew about the past.

Since then, nationally applied criteria have dictated how history departments have to assess their pupils. Although there have been important changes within the structure of the mechanism, a system based on Level Descriptors is still deemed the most effective way to gauge levels progression within history. At the end of each key stage, every pupil is given a Level, representing their progress over the course of that key stage. Given the range of concepts which feature within the subject, attributing a single level to a pupil is no easy task, and the great strength of the NC Levels is that they help the teacher gain a general sense of how a pupil is doing at that particular transition stage. This, in turn, is helpful to pastoral staff and school leaders, trying to put together a picture of how cohorts are doing in different subjects, and how individual pupils are doing across the curriculum. It also provides a neat summary for parents as to how their child is doing, in different subjects, which may influence their subject choices for the next stage in their education.

Whilst the NC model of progression does have its uses, both individual components and indeed the construct itself have come under intense criticism, most notably from Lee and Shemilt (2003). Whilst they accept that the Levels allow teachers to make 'best fit' judgements about a pupil's overall level of historical understanding, they challenge the principle underpinning the hierarchical Level structure, arguing that children do not progress at the same rate in each of the different concepts. Their research found that a pupil might demonstrate excellent awareness of causation, but may struggle to evaluate evidence. The NC does not make provision for such subtle distinctions, instead assuming that all aspects of conceptual understanding progress in tandem.

By way of alternative, Lee and Shemilt advocate an alternative approach to assessing progression. Teachers need to identify progression through each of the second-order concepts separately. Only in this way can different rates of progression through each concept be recognized and responded to. In order to do this, teachers have to construct levels of progression for

Stage 1:	Little understanding of causation. Pupils do not recognize links between actions or events and consequences.
Stage 2:	Some recognition of links between causes and effects. Likely to identify single cause, and to state that one type of cause just leads to the same type of consequence.
Stage 3:	Awareness that events have a multitude of causes.
Stage 4:	Able to confidently distinguish between type of cause. Able to distinguish between intended and unintended cause.
Stage 5:	Able to explain how causes interact, and to identify most significant causes.
Stage 6:	Able to construct a clear hierarchy of cause and consequence.

Figure 2.9 Model of progression for assessing understanding of causation

each concept which are not strictly hierarchical and not linked to age. An example of such a model of progression is provided in Figure 2.9.

Teachers therefore need to plan to develop pupil understanding of the different concepts across the key stages, and the different units. Assessment of the concepts needs to be built into existing schemes of work, so they do not appear as an artificial 'bolt-on'. This is likely to involve graduated build-up, perhaps starting with the establishment of a secure grasp of the narrative, before introducing smaller tasks related to the concept being assessed, and culminating in an extended task. This task need not be a formal written assessment, but, as Fullard and Dacey (2008) demonstrate, a range of activities can be used to assess understanding.

◆ *APP and the future of assessment*

Assessing Pupil Progress (see, for example, Qualifications and Curriculum Authority, 2009) is an attempt to bridge the gap between the two most common forms of assessments carried out in schools: those carried out on a daily basis in the classroom, and those performed on a more public stage at transition points in pupils' educational career (e.g. KS3 levelling, GCSE, AS levels). By introducing the notion of 'periodic' assessments, teachers will be able to compare the performance of their pupils against nationally established criteria, and hopefully gain a clearer insight into areas of the curriculum or particular skills where individual pupils may have weaknesses. In short, the intention is to create a more rigorous strand to AfL, where hard evidence is used to support learning. As far as day-to-day assessment is concerned:

- learning objectives should be made explicit and shared with pupils;
- peer and self-assessment should be used;
- pupils should be engaged in their learning and given immediate feedback.

Period assessment requires:

- a broader view of progress across subject for teacher and learner;
- use of national standards in the classroom;
- improvements to medium-term curriculum planning.

Finally, transition assessment should involve:

- formal recognition of pupils' achievement;
- reports to parents/carers and then teacher(s);
- use of external tests or tasks.

The Qualifications and Curriculum Authority (2009) believe that the introduction of APP will develop 'teachers' confidence and expertise in assessment by providing a common framework for sharing and discussing the evidence they have of learners' progress'.

Although history teachers will not have to grapple with APP 2010, their colleagues in English, Science, MFL and ICT have already integrated it into their assessment programmes. The experiences of these subjects offers some clues as to what historians are likely to face when APP comes on stream for them. At the time of writing, no draft materials for history had been published, but experiences from the APP History pilot are outlined in *Teaching History* (December 2009).

Following on from the implementation of a new National Curriculum in 2008, many teachers will be concerned by the 'arrival' of new assessment focuses and levels. The 2009 pilot was based upon three Assessment Focuses (with links to NC Key Concepts):

AF1: Thinking Historically (KS3 Key Concepts: Chronology; Diversity; Change; Causation)

AF2: Exploring Interpretations (KS3 Key Concepts: Significance;
   Interpetations)
AF3: Historical Enquiry (KS3 Key Processes: Enquiry; Evidence;
   Communication).

At first glance, the suggested programme for performing APP does little to alleviate fears that teachers are likely to be placed under a huge amount of pressure. However, experiences of teachers across those subject areas where APP has already been introduced suggest that, after a period of adjustment, teachers found it reasonably straightforward to internalize levels and Assessment Focuses, whilst the overall benefits of assessing pupil progress in this manner seemed to outweigh many concerns about added teacher workload.

The process of carrying out APP is divided into six steps:

1. Over a period of time, decide on the outcomes to be assessed and generate evidence of pupils' attainment from day-to-day teaching and learning.
2. Review an appropriate range of evidence. This should include different types of task, and include classroom contributions.
3. Highlight assessment criteria for which there is evidence.
4. Use the pupil's developing profile of learning to decide upon a level and sub-level.
5. Moderate assessments.
6. Make any necessary adjustments to planning, teaching and intervention.

The guidance recommends that, in order to gain the most accurate picture of pupil progress, teachers use a variety of tasks spread over the course of several months: written tasks, role-play, group discussion, video productions, etc. This should also have a motivational impact on the pupils. If they are aware that 'everything counts', then they will see each lesson as an essential part of the process of improving at history, and hopefully appreciate the rewards of seeing all of their contributions formally validated.

Tasks

1. Perhaps working with a colleague, choose one of the following second-order concepts, and devise a model of progression for KS3 pupils. Decide the process by which you will research and construct

the model, then provide a summary of the different levels. You may also want to read relevant articles from *Teaching History*, such as Oliver Knight's in issue 131, June 2008 or the whole of issue 115, June 2004. (http://www.history.org.uk/resources/secondary_resources_12.html)

Empathy
Causation
Change and continuity
Evidence

2. Select one class that you teach to experiment with different types of formative assessment. Introduce comment-based marking for a whole topic, and evaluate the impact it has had on pupil performance. Are they more motivated, or do they prefer receiving grades? Is there evidence that pupils are starting to incorporate your suggestions for improvement into their work? One way to monitor the results of this experiment is to keep a brief diary, where you can record the effects of the strategy.

Teaching source skills

3

Using historical sources

◆ *Why should I use historical evidence in my teaching?*

Until the early 1970s, most history teaching was driven by first-order concepts, i.e. what happened, when it happened, and who made it happen. History was a study of events, and the complicated, interesting stuff was left to undergraduates and professional historians.

However, a gradual process, which saw such Piagetian notions of academic capability rejected, has seen history teaching evolve to a point where second-order concepts such as cause and consequence and interpretation are placed on an equal footing with knowledge and understanding. The 2007 National Curriculum identifies 'interpretation' as one of the key concepts which 'underpin the study of history', whilst 'historical enquiry' and 'using evidence' are two of the three key processes, defined as 'the essential skills and processes in history that pupils need to learn to make progress'. 'Historical enquiry' relates to using evidence, as pupils are expected to select and deploy evidence to test their own hypotheses.

Apart from a statutory requirement to teach evidence, why should we devote so much of our time teaching it?

The most fundamental reason is that it can be highly enjoyable. Rather than receiving someone else's take on the past, whether it be the teacher, textbook author or documentary maker, pupils can begin to practise 'real' history, and can make judgements about historical events based on the evidence at their disposal. Evidence work is, therefore, at the centre of what historians do to construct a picture of what happened, why and with results. Pupils can only really understand the furore surrounding Cromwell's actions in Drogheda and Wexford in 1649 by looking at documentary evidence from the time chronicling not only the reactions from both sides, but also the rules of engagement used at that time.

From a historical perspective, it is not possible to build up a picture of the past without considering the nature, origins and purpose of evidence. The earlier approach, taking 'history as a story', fails to equip pupils with the tools required to consider multiple and conflicting versions of the same event, thus making it difficult for them to understand what did indeed take place. It also assumes that historians know everything there is to know about events in history and that there is an agreed version of 'the truth'. Any casual study of a Year 8 textbook will demonstrate the fallacy of that belief.

Being able to handle large amounts of 'evidence' is also one of the generic life skills which history helps to develop within the school curriculum. No matter what the occupation, people frequently have to process, analyse and evaluate conflicting information, and the perception of history as being predominantly an 'evidence-processing' subject partially explains why source skills are an important feature of the National Curriculum.

◆ What are the most effective ways to use evidence in my lessons?

Perhaps a key point to make here is that historical sources can, and should, be used within most lessons. Even where the focus is not source skills, they can still be effectively included to illuminate sections of the lesson or to illustrate contemporary attitudes to an event.

However, this section focuses on three specific uses of source material: to introduce a lesson or topic; to test hypotheses; and to be integrated into extended pieces of writing.

Sources as 'initial stimulus material'

Rob Phillips devotes a whole chapter of his book, *Reflective Teaching of History 11–18*, to what he terms 'initial stimulus material' (Phillips, 2002). By this he means the use of sources to engage pupil interest, to create an enquiry or hypothesis, and to outline aims and objectives. The chief advantage of this approach is that it creates something 'known' in the pupils' mind which can be referred back to in future lessons.

For example, if a class of Year 10 pupils were about to start an exploration of the causes of the October 1917 Revolution in Russia, the enquiry could start with a short clip from Eisenstein's 1922 masterpiece, *Oktober* (if you cannot obtain a copy, the desired clip can be found at http://www.youtube.com/watch?v=x0QAjpeosgU), which shows the main assault on the Winter Palace. After showing the clip, ask the class a series of open questions, designed to assess understanding of what they have just seen and to link into the main themes of the enquiry. Such questions might begin with:

- What have you just seen?

From there, the questions will push the pupils to develop their thinking about the clip. . .

- Do you think that this was a significant event?
- Did it appear to be a well-supported event?
- Could you tell who may not have welcomed the event?
- Were there any clues as to the attitude of the film-maker to the event?

The next stage of the lesson would be to demystify the origin of the source and its links to the topic. As a means of establishing the lines of enquiry, the teacher could ask the class to come up with their own key questions. In this case, the goal of the teacher might be to lead the pupils to a broad enquiry testing the hypothesis that the Bolshevik Revolution was a product of a popular uprising.

A slightly different approach could see the pupils enter a room with the source already playing, or presented on the screen. As mentioned in the previous chapter, one of my most effective starters to a topic occurs at the start of the Year 11 course on Nazi Germany 1930–1939. The pupils enter a darkened room, with the introduction to Leni Riefenstahl's *Olympia* playing on the screen. The pupils are quickly engrossed by the morphing of classical statues into athletes, and the journey of the Olympic torch from Greece, across Europe, to Berlin, where the footage switches to the opening ceremony. As with the *Oktober* clip, my first question is open and general: 'what have you just seen?'. Gradually, I get to the point where I want to know what kind of images are being presented by the film-maker, why she would want to do this, what the images say about the regime which hosted the Games. This leads to the first main enquiry focusing on the Nazi rise to power.

One of my newer experiments with sources as stimulus material involves a nursery rhyme, 'Little Jack Horner':

Little Jack Horner sat in the corner
Eating his Christmas pie,
He put in his thumb and pulled out a plum
And said 'What a good boy am I!'

Whilst it does not lead into a large topic, it provides a way into a mini-enquiry based around the dissolution of the monasteries. The introduction is very simple; I ask the class if they know what the nursery rhyme is about. As hardly anyone can provide a correct answer, I then ask them to think about the language of the source, whether it should be taken literally, or whether there is anything in it which might be representative of something else. After allowing a few minutes for several valiant interpretations, I explain the origins of the rhyme. 'Jack' is supposed to be the steward of the Bishop of Glastonbury, who was instructed to take a bribe to Henry VIII consisting of 12 title deeds to various manorial estates. This was to prevent the King closing down the last remaining abbey in Somerset, Glastonbury. According to the story, the steward stole one of the deeds, hidden in a pie, before ratting on his bishop to the King. This is the point when I ask the pupils to draw up their own enquiry questions, which are reviewed and filtered in the plenary session. Subsequent lessons focus on the origins of the dissolution, reaction from Henry's opponents, and the fate of the monks, nuns and buildings (when it makes perfect sense to bring back 'Little Jack' to remind the pupils about one such building). This stimulus could also be used to launch a big enquiry into the English Reformation, as it throw up something strange, new, yet likely to arouse the curiosity of the pupils and stick in their minds.

Phillips provides a handy hints list to make the use of stimulus material more effective. These include the following:

- Maintain an air of mystery about the source. By not providing much in the way of provenance, you can enhance the curiosity of the pupils, and further guarantee their interest in the enquiry.
- Plan your questioning in advance. Questions have to be both realistic (in the sense that they are accessible to all the class) and likely to lead the pupils towards the lesson's objectives.
- Do not overestimate the extent of prior knowledge or understanding of the source.

- Use a range of sources as stimulus material. Films, photographs, portraits, oral accounts, reading from a novel or diary, are just some of the types of source which can deliver an effective stimulus effect. It is tempting to overlook the use of a textbook, but most modern books contain a wealth of fascinating source material.

Sources as evidence

As indicated earlier, using sources as pieces of historical evidence not only humanizes the subject, but also allows pupils to model the work of professional historians. In the process, they also get the opportunity to develop a range of skills including communication, observation, deduction, interpretation, and questioning.

There are several important ways in which you are likely to use evidence, The first is *analysing its utility*. Assessing the usefulness of a source is a popular and valuable task at Key Stage 3 and GCSE, but it is important to bear in mind that a source's utility will vary according to the purpose for which it is being assessed. Therefore, a copy of a trench map might be more useful than a music hall song when trying to explain why Britain found it so hard to break the stalemate on the Western Front, yet the music hall song would be probably be more useful when examining what life in the trenches was like for British soldiers.

When analysing utility, it is important to consider both the content and provenance of the source. Figure 3.1 provides a template for introducing source utility tasks.

The danger with this approach is that it takes the attention of the pupil away from the source and towards the table. Whilst the exercise is a practical way to develop source skills, it is to be hoped that pupils will be encouraged to engage more directly with the actual sources over a longer period of time. One way to help this come about is to photocopy the original source and write targeted questions either on the photocopy or at the side. With my Year 8 pupils I always use the 'Ditchley portrait' of Queen Elizabeth I (by Marcus Gheeraerts the Younger; this can be viewed in the National Portrait Gallery, or on their website, http://www.npg.org.uk/collections/search/portrait.php?LinkID=mp01452&page=2&rNo=10&role=sit) as part of our investigation into how successfully she tackled the problems which faced her during her reign. In the margins, I have written questions asking the pupils to both describe what they can see in the portrait, and comment on the significance of certain aspects of the portrait (e.g. the different weather conditions portrayed).

How useful is source 'A' to a historian studying the lack of a breakthrough on the Western Front 1915–1917?				
	Strengths of the source for a historian studying the lack of a breakthrough on the Western Front		Limitations of the source to a historian studying the lack of a breakthrough on the Western Front	Conclusion
Source A	Content *What does it tell you about the reasons for the lack of a break-through on the Western Front?*	Provenance *Add a brief comment whether you can 'trust' the source (NB even unreliable sources can still be useful...)*	Content *What doesn't it mention which you know is important?*	Provenance

Figure 3.1 Source utility template

This leads into a discussion about the uses of this source to historians assessing Elizabeth's reign, and how far we can trust this as a piece of evidence.

The second way you are likely to use evidence is in *evaluating its reliability*. It is probably fair to say that the study of historical evidence has moved on from a time when detection of bias or evaluation of a source's reliability was the main feature of source work. This is undoubtedly a good thing, as it illustrates the increasing skill level of pupils in handling evidence (i.e. their awareness of 'bias' is built into more sophisticated tasks such as cross-referencing or study of source utility), and represents a step away from a slightly reductionist approach to source work, characterized by an obsession with the reliability of a source.

Instead, the twin concepts of bias and reliability are used to gauge different attitudes amongst people in the past, and as a way of discriminating between pieces of evidence in broader enquiries. The first use, examining attitudes, is one which is most often overlooked when students analyse reliability. Coming across something they regard as unreliable, they can be quick to dismiss its worth to a historian, ignoring the key point that seemingly 'unreliable' pieces of evidence are invaluable as evidence about attitudes at a given time.

Good practice when looking at the reliability of sources in the classroom suggests that (a) the provenance, (b) the content of the source, and (c) the pupils' own knowledge of the period being studied need to be analysed in order to make a comprehensive judgement. To cover all these areas, you might want to implement the following question structure:

- What is its *nature*? Is it a photograph, memoir, novel? What is the balance of fact and opinion? Does it use lots of adjectives to exaggerate its viewpoint? Will the nature of the source affect your judgement about its trustworthiness?
- What is its origin? Who produced it? What do you know about them? When was it produced? Is that date important? What else was happening at that time which might have influenced the attitude of the author?
- What was its purpose? Why was it made? Who was the intended audience? Was it for public or private consumption? Was the intention to inform, entertain, educate, or indoctrinate?

The third use of evidence involves *cross-referencing sources.* If historians want to build up as complete a picture as possible as to what happened in the past, they need to consider different pieces of evidence. If they only look at a single piece of evidence, there will be no guarantee that this source is accurate, or provides a full account. Cross-referencing is therefore an important historical skill, in order to evaluate the reliability of other sources, and to piece together bits of evidence to make up a credible version of past events.

At a basic level, pupils can be asked to identify areas of disagreement between two similar *types* of sources, before moving on to a greater number and variety of sources as they become more adept at performing this type of exercise.

There are different ways in which they can be helped to develop this particular skill. Figure 3.2 provides a template for such development.

A more conventional and more detailed approach would require the pupil to analyse what each source had to say about specific features of a period. This method can help older students make sense of more complex sources, as it provides a clear focus for their research, and allows for a more straightforward comparison of content. Figure 3.3 provides a template for this, using the different accounts of Pope Urban's proclamation at Clermont in 1095 as an example.

	A		B		Conclusion: which source is closest to C? Refer to the provenance to explain why
How far do sources A and B agree with source C about the role of Hitler in attracting voters to the NSDAP 1930–1932?					
C	Agree	Disagree	Agree	Disagree	

Figure 3.2. Source cross-referencing table

	What did Urban say about…			
	Atonement for sins	Jerusalem	Protecting Christians from infidels	Coming to the assistance of Emperor Alexius
Fulcher of Chartres 1100–1106				
Robert the Monk c.1106				
Baldric of Dol 1108–1110				
Guibert of Nogent c.1108				

Figure 3.3 Comparison of content

For teachers who really want to experiment with cross-referencing, role-play and hot-seating can be used to add a bit of colour to the enquiry. One of the best forms of role-play I have come across was the 'Enclosure Game', a fully resourced unit which allowed pupils to follow the effects of enclosure on a village over a period of 50 years. Within the game, every pupil was allocated a character, with background notes, and a certain amount of land in the village. The focus for the early lessons was a debate over whether the village should enclose. Over time, the effects of enclosure on the different villagers meant that attitudes and lives of the villagers changed. This was a useful evidence task as it allowed the pupils to explore the different attitudes of real characters from the past, and to compare and contrast their differing perspectives. In this way, they were able to explain how far enclosure was beneficial to most people in the countryside. Although the game is now unavailable, the theory behind it is straightforward enough to adapt to most periods of history.

Hot-seating differs from this type of role-play activity, as it can involve the pupils either coming to a lesson fully briefed and ready to be a figure from history, or coming to the lesson prepared to interrogate someone (the teacher?) about the attitudes of a figure from history. With both role-play and hot-seating, the activities should lead into a discussion of why the various characters held those viewpoints, and whether any common ground existed.

One further tip is to encourage the pupils to see that sources rarely agree with each other completely. They should demonstrate this in their answers by using phrases such as 'there is partial agreement', 'they agree with each other to an extent', or 'for the most part they agree, but there are key differences'...

The final use of evidence is in *helping to answer a bigger enquiry question*. Evidence can be used to support an argument at KS3 right through to A level. With younger pupils, you might ask them to assess how far a piece of evidence supports a particular viewpoint. Adding a greater range of sources, with conflicting perspectives, makes the task more complex to the point where a GCSE question might ask: 'Germany was defeated in World War I because of the entry of the USA into the war. Using the sources and your own knowledge, say how far you agree with this statement.' This question requires the pupil to use the sources to support and challenge a statement, and make fairly simple judgements about the trustworthiness of a source. Pupils always find it tricky linking the content of the source both to their own

Sources which agree with the statement	Own knowledge which illustrates points raised in the source	Comment on reliability	Links to other sources?
Conclusion			

Figure 3.4 GCSE-style evaluation table

knowledge and to other sources. However, being able to perform these skills is likely to be rewarded by very high marks.

To help pupils prepare for a task of this kind, an 'evaluation table' can help them structure their response (see Figure 3.4).

For pupils in the 16–18 range, they may be asked to use a range of primary and secondary sources to evaluate a particular interpretation of events. The added challenge at this level is not only to skilfully integrate the sources into an argument, but to recognize the interpretations which each source supports. Greater credit is awarded for the ability to cross-reference sources as well. For example, 'Using the sources and your own knowledge, assess how far the development of an arms race was responsible for the origins and continuation of the Cold War 1945–1960'. A question like this requires students to do an awful lot with the source material in a short period of time, and they should be encouraged to really engage with it. They could use different coloured pens to link the source to others which it either agrees with or challenges, and relevant supporting contextual knowledge should be scribbled in the margin next to it. Students can be afraid to 'deface' an examination paper, but they will evaluate its content more effectively if they take the time to annotate it before writing their response.

◆ What are the pitfalls of using evidence in my teaching?

Ironically, given its importance to the subject, doing source work can be laid open to the charge of not doing 'proper' history. After all, when the focus is on processes, rather than historical content, pupils could be learning about anything. In order to avoid this, and to ensure sources are used effectively, you should be aware of the following common flaws in teaching historical sources:

1. Making a false and meaningless distinction between primary and secondary sources. Too often in examinations, pupils assess the reliability or utility of a source simply through reference to the time it was produced, 'he was there at the time, so it must be more reliable' and 'it is written by a historian, so it must be accurate' being two of the most common generalized statements produced by some pupils. When they do this, pupils are forgetting the key principles of good evidence work, outlined above.

2. Providing inaccessible material. If pupils cannot understand the language, or fail to pick up on the subtleties of a cartoon, then they will not be able to evaluate it. It is the teacher's job to make the evidence accessible to the audience for which it is intended. Provide a glossary, amend the language in the text, draw attention to less obvious elements in a picture – anything that will enable the pupil to understand and analyse its true meaning.

3. Do not detach the sources from their historical context. Encouraging students to generate stock phrases such as 'it's a photograph of the event, so it must be reliable' or, conversely, 'the photographer will have decided what to include and what to leave out of the picture, so we cannot trust his version of events' removes any element of history from the task. Instead, pupils should be encouraged at all times to relate the content of the source and provenance to what they know has happened.

4. It can be tempting for teachers to devote too much time to looking at a source in isolation, rather than using to pursue a particular enquiry. Whilst it is tempting to spend hours decoding Lenin's April Theses line by line, the benefit to the pupils might be less than you would like to think! One of the main themes of this chapter is that evidence work

has to have a purpose, and the pupils must know why they are looking at a particular source, and how it fits into the bigger enquiry. Without this focus, the quality of source analysis is likely to be superficial, and interest in the material will not be sustained. Above all, without reference to context or an enquiry question, the pupils will not be doing challenging history, just doing more sources.

Given that history at GCSE requires students to be proficient in using sources, and that the questions tend to isolate singular methods of looking at sources (i.e. utility, cross-referencing, reliability), it is more difficult for teachers to avoid teaching source skills separate from the rest of the course. If they do not, then they risk underpreparing their classes for important external examinations; if they do, they may risk demotivating pupils through repetition of mechanical procedures. In order to send the students into the examination with the skills to tackle source papers, whilst keeping them interested, you need to maintain a focus on the enquiry-based approach, albeit with greater reference to evidence throughout the enquiry. If the source skills appear integral to the unit, and are presented in a variety of ways, the pupils should retain their interest in the subject and achieve their desired grades in the examination.

◆ *Where can I access sources on the web?*

Internet Medieval Source Book
http://www.fordham.edu/halsall/sbook.html

Internet Modern History Source Book
http://www.fordham.edu/halsall/mod/modsbook.html

Medieval images (provided by University of Leicester)
http://picasaweb.google.com/leicmrc/Leicmedres#

National Archives Education Service
http://www.nationalarchives.gov.uk/education/
default.htm?source=ddmenu_research3

'Eyes on the Prize' (accompanying site to PBS series)
http://www.pbs.org/wgbh/amex/eyesontheprize/

Cold War International History Project
http://www.wilsoncenter.org/
index.cfm?fuseaction=topics.home&topic_id=1409

The Cold War Files
http://www.wilsoncenter.org/coldwarfiles/
index.cfm?fuseaction=home.flash

First World War   http://www.firstworldwar.com

Trenches on the Web   http://www.worldwar1.com

National Portrait Gallery history section
http://www.npg.org.uk/learning/digital/history.php

Online version of the Bayeux Tapestry
http://members.tripod.com/~mr_sedivy/med_bay.html

Life of an industrial worker during the Industrial Revolution
http://www.victorianweb.org/history/workers2.html

BBC WW2 People's War
http://www.bbc.co.uk/ww2peopleswar/

BBC Special Operations Executive online exhibition
http://www.bbc.co.uk/history/worldwars/wwtwo/soe_gallery.shtml

Seventeen moments in Soviet history
http://soviethistory.org/

Cuban Missile Crisis Film Archive   http://www.teachers.tv/video/2531

Teacher's site to accompany CNN/ BBC *Cold War* series
http://cgi.turnerlearning.com/cnn/coldwar/cw_start.html

Digital History (US resources)   http://www.digitalhistory.uh.edu/

Interpretations

◆ *What are interpretations?*

It is not difficult to confuse historical evidence and interpretations. After all, we tend to include 'secondary sources' in the general category 'evidence', whilst historians obviously rely heavily on the available evidence whilst constructing their interpretations. However, as the National Curriculum makes very clear, as a teacher you have to be able to distinguish between them, and present them to pupils in different ways.

So, how do we distinguish between them? The most important distinction lies in the way that they are created. Whereas evidence is often created without consideration for its future historical value, and tends not to be the product of an extensive research process, interpretations deliberately represent the past in a certain way, depending on a range of historical sources, and contemporary attitudes to influence its creation.

Our use of evidence and interpretations differs too. We use sources as part of broader enquiries, and within that process we have to evaluate their reliability and use as evidence for tackling that enquiry. Interpretations, however, are evaluated not so much for what they have to say about the past, as for what they can tell us about how and why they were created. So, whilst sources will be used to answer a question, we will look at interpretations to understand why different historians have answered that question in different ways. As an illustration, an enquiry into whether King John was a bad king would not be a valid topic for the study of interpretations as it will involve original sources, as well as historians' perspectives. However, if the enquiry was focused on how historians have judged King John, then it *would* be a study of interpretations.

◆ *What are the most effective ways to teach interpretations?*

Clearly, there is not one single way to teach interpretations. However, the following is a basic model for delivering a unit on interpretations, which is based on my experience and the work of Haydn et al. (2001) and Phillips (2002).

- Start by explaining the purpose of studying interpretations. You will be looking at history in a slightly different way: studying why someone has presented their take on the subject in a certain way, rather than examining what happened and why. In the process, pupils will learn about the work of historians and that fact there is more than one way of thinking about the subject. They should also see that interpretations of past events or individuals frequently change over time.
- The next stage should involve providing the pupils with background about the topic. As with other forms of evidence, pupils will only be able to conduct meaningful investigations into interpretations if they can make comparisons with what they know actually happened.
- So that they can gain an understanding of the subjective nature of the subject, ask the pupils to write their own short interpretations of the event under consideration. A follow-up discussion could compare interpretations and outline the process they used to create their version of events.
- You could then present them with a wide range of interpretations, of different types and perspectives. This is a great way of presenting the different methods people use to present history, and reinforcing the earlier point about the changing nature of interpretations. A

good starting point is to provide several types of interpretation on a topic and ask the pupils at first to identify the viewpoints which agree with each other. This can lead into a task exploring why they might agree/differ. (Figure 3.5 outlines possible types of interpretation which can be used.)

What types of interpretations could I use?

★ Historical novels
★ Old textbooks
★ Films (e.g. *Cromwell, Elizabeth, A Man for All Seasons, The Lion in Winter, Restoration, JFK, The Green Berets.* The Internet Movie Database at http://www.imdb.com/ is a handy source of information about writers, directors, etc.)
★ Historical TV documentaries
★ Paintings
★ Poetry (poets such as Wilfred Owen and Siegfried Sassoon present a very slanted view of the First World War)
★ Music (folk songs often deal with historical events. http://folkmusic.about.com/od/toptens/tp/Top10Protest.htm outlines 10 relatively modern classics)
★ Children's history books
★ Museums (perhaps incorporate a field visit into the study)
★ Preserved battlefields sites and castles
★ Websites (the potential perils of relying too much on Wikipedia could be explored by evaluating their page on the Industrial Revolution. I'm not suggesting that it is flawed in any way, but it could prove a useful exercise in interrogating commonly accepted interpretations of historical events: http://en.wikipedia.org/wiki/Industrial_Revolution)

Figure 3.5 Types of interpretation

- Exploring why sources might have similar or different viewpoints requires the pupils to ask questions about the different interpretations. This could be presented as a list of questions, questionnaire style, or in a grid. Suggestions for questions are provided in Figure 3.6. You will have to provide further information to make this work. Background notes on authors, glossaries to ease accessibility, and possibility notes on the time when the interpretations may all be required.

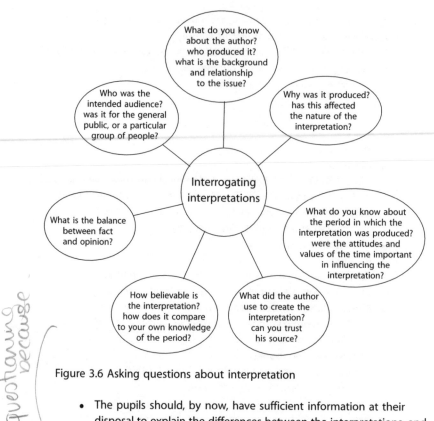

What do you know about the author? who produced it? what is the background and relationship to the issue?

Who was the intended audience? was it for the general public, or a particular group of people?

Why was it produced? has this affected the nature of the interpretation?

Interrogating interpretations

What is the balance between fact and opinion?

What do you know about the period in which the interpretation was produced? were the attitudes and values of the time important in influencing the interpretation?

How believable is the interpretation? how does it compare to your own knowledge of the period?

What did the author use to create the interpretation? can you trust his source?

questioning because [handwritten margin note]

Figure 3.6 Asking questions about interpretation

- The pupils should, by now, have sufficient information at their disposal to explain the differences between the interpretations, and why the interpretations have developed over time. You could develop this stage of the unit by asking them to decide which of the interpretations is the most credible.
- If you want a task which assesses understanding of interpretations and how they are constructed, you could choose one of the following:
  - Present one interpretation, and get the pupils to challenge its version of events. (Extra credit should be given to those who can go beyond the conclusions of the interpretation, and explain its flaws through reference to the factors which might have influenced the author.)
  - Write a letter to a director criticizing his version of a particular event.
  - Produce a proposal for the Department of Culture for the development of a new museum about the suffragette movement. Explain what interpretation you intend to present,

and the type of resources which might feature.

- Match the author to the interpretation.
- 'Spot the fact' in an interpretation.
- Role-play around different interpretations. This could work as a fictional TV panel show. Each 'guest' represents a viewpoint and is interrogated by other members of the class (the audience) about their perspective.
- Use a free animation package such as www.xtranormal.com to create an animated dialogue between two fictional historians
- Use a more sophisticated presentation package such as www.prezi.com to either present evidence to support an interpretation, or to present a summary of the main interpretations.

Tasks

1 After you have taught a unit on interpretations, it might be worthwhile reviewing your approach. Your review might focus on the following issues:

- How much background knowledge did you provide?
- When and how did you provide the background knowledge?
- Were the interpretations suitable for the task, the pupils' age, and ability range?
- How did you manage progression through the unit? Did you provide sufficient guidance on questioning the interpretations?
- Was your method of assessing progression suitable?
- In summary, how could you improve your approach to interpretations in future?

2 Devise a standalone ICT-based task where pupils have to engage directly with a source to assess its usefulness. Assuming the pupils are pursuing an enquiry into the collapse of the Russian monarchy in February 1917, choose a visual image from http:// uk.images.search.yahoo.com/search/images?_adv_prop=image &fr=mcafee&va=february+revolution+1917&sz=all, and copy it into a PowerPoint presentation. Ask the pupils to insert and fill two textboxes to identify the strengths and two for the limitations of the source's content. They should then add a final textbox where they comment on the provenance of the source.

Inclusion

4

Inclusion refers to all pupils having the opportunity to access and achieve in meaningful educational contexts, irrespective of learning need. A number of factors have contributed to the growing importance of inclusion to teachers, including immigration, incorporation of more pupils with special educational needs (SEN) into mainstream education, and a renewed focus on a more personalized approach to education. There is a statutory responsibility on schools to respond to different educational needs by setting suitable learning challenges, responding to pupils' diverse learning needs and overcoming potential barriers to learning and assessment for individuals and groups of pupils.

This chapter concentrates on three groups of pupils, whose particular needs require teachers to develop suitable intervention strategies in order to help them fulfil their potential. These groups are: pupils with special educational needs; those who have English as an additional language; and gifted and talented pupils. In each case, I outline the impediments to learning, and consider the lessons of theory and recent experience to offer practical steps to help these pupils.

Pupils with special educational needs

The relationship between history and SEN has not always been a happy one. When increased focus was placed on meeting the needs of pupils with learning difficulties, history lagged behind other subjects when it came down to resources, methods of teaching, and even the accessibility of the National Curriculum Attainment Targets. Even today, when there has been considerable progression in the teaching of history to SEN pupils, parental confidence in schools' ability to support SEN pupils is not encouraging (TES, 2009).

◆ *What are the barriers to learning history for pupils with special educational needs?*

The first barrier is the nature of educational need which a pupil might have. Your school is likely to have a special educational needs coordinator (SENCO), and you should always consult this person if you have any concerns about a pupil who has an SEN or you suspect has a so far undiagnosed SEN.

Although you will not be expected to have a detailed knowledge of different learning disabilities, the main ones which you will encounter in the classroom are:

- Dyslexia. Dyslexia is a disability which leads to people to develop a very different way of thinking and learning. Although dyslexics may display very strong signs of being creative, or orally fluent, they tend to struggle with concentration, organization, following instructions, sequencing, spelling and processing.
- Dyspraxia (or developmental coordination disorder). Dyspraxic children struggle with coordination of their movement, but will usually have further related problems, including heightened sensory awareness, reading at speed, and expressing themselves verbally in a clear and coherent fashion.
- Attention deficit (hyperactivity) disorder. People with ADD/ADHD tend to be energetic and imaginative, yet they will also have a short attention span and be very talkative, disruptive, socially clumsy, aggressive, inconsiderate, or restless.
- Autism. People with autistic spectrum disorders show signs of having difficulty developing relationships with others, and can appear to be badly behaved.
- Asperger's: this is a form of autism, defined by three areas of 'difference'. These result in sufferers struggling with social interaction, picking up on non-verbal forms of communication, and empathy.

Until the early 1970s, the main barrier to learning was thought to be the child itself. Whilst all children were thought to struggle with 'adult' concepts such as change, continuity and causation, the particular difficulties faced by SEN pupils were thought to be insurmountable. However, as educational theory moved away from Piategetian models, greater emphasis was placed on the environment in which children learned as obstructing their progress. The barriers outlined are those that exist solely within the classroom.

Accessing the material

The primary issue preventing pupils from accessing historical materials is language. Whether they are reading passages in a textbook, considering historical sources, or listening to teacher exposition, the complexity of historical language impedes progression right from the start. History is a literate subject, and teachers will, perhaps unknowingly, present concepts and processes to pupils without appreciating how difficult they may appear to some pupil in their class. For example, teaching the clash between Charles I and Parliament is likely to involve some discussion of the 'divine right of kings', and the subtle distinction between power and authority which it encompasses. Similarly, a study of religious life in the Middle Ages presents enormous challenges to a pupil with an SEN, with its emphasis on quite abstract concepts such as beliefs and traditions.

The nature and extent of writing in a textbook can also create problems. The need to provide a degree of contextual information about a period or event often results in the production of text-heavy resources. When the text can also be littered with reference to the type of concepts outlined above, the difficulties multiply.

Haydn et al. (2001) suggest that poor teaching methods are one of the largest obstacles to good learning amongst SEN pupils. These include overuse of 'teacher talk', especially when there is a large amount of new material or highly complex language is being used. Pupils with short attention spans may therefore find it difficult access those parts of the lesson where the teacher is explaining the most important parts of a task, thus preventing them understanding what is required of them.

Communicating their historical understanding

Phillips (2008) outlines the difficulty which a need for secure conceptual understanding creates for SEN pupils' ability to communicate effectively, either on paper or verbally.

The most common way for pupils to demonstrate understanding will be on paper, yet written tasks, especially extended written tasks, are often the most problematic for SEN pupils. For some, the issue will be linking what they have read or heard to what they have to write, resulting in chunks of a response which appear to be copied directly from the textbook. Others may find it difficult to analyse or explain events, offering instead a narrative account. Even those who are able to adopt an analytical framework can struggle to develop arguments because they cannot identify the appropriate supporting evidence. As a result, their responses tend to be assertive and lacking sufficient depth.

◆ How can these barriers be overcome?

In spite of these barriers to learning, the Qualifications and Curriculum Development Agency website strongly asserts the benefits for SEN pupils which can be accrued from studying history. History presents opportunities to:

> develop knowledge and understanding of the sequences, routines and chronological patterns that make up their world

- develop an understanding of their personal history alongside understanding about events in the world and what shapes them
- develop knowledge and understanding of how people lived in other times and how those times were different from today
- experience a range of representations of the past
- use a range of evidence to find out about the past.

(http://www.qcda.gov.uk/1891.aspx)

Before setting foot in the classroom, a teacher will have both legal and school-based obligations regarding their treatment of SEN pupils. The Disability Discrimination Act and the SEN code of practice already include a duty on schools to cater for children with additional needs, whilst the policy of individual schools will also affect what procedures the teacher will have to follow.

For example, a teaching assistant (TA) may already have been assigned to a pupil with SEN. If so, the teacher needs to ensure that he understands the role of the TA in the classroom, and that the TA is aware in advance what will be expected of her in each lesson. The school may also have devised an individual education plan for the SEN pupil, which the teacher should be aware of and able to incorporate into his planning.

Whilst learning disabilities are complex, and do not manifest themselves in exactly the same way in every sufferer, teachers in all subjects can make the learning experience of SEN pupils less daunting by performing certain simple and general tasks:

- Allow the use of a laptop, if desired. Discuss how work will be presented to you: email; homework area on the network; or printed off?
- Ensure all instructions are delivered clearly, and presented on the board.
- When on task, check the progress of certain pupils regularly.

- Any homework tasks need to be presented on the board at the start of the lesson, allowing plenty of time for pupils to write them down. If necessary, a printed version could be given to pupils with poor organization or literacy skills.
- Make good use of handouts. Possibly even hand out additional notes as background.
- Vary the nature of activity. As a rule, short tasks are better for many SEN pupils, but any pupil will easily become bored if expected to so the same thing every lesson.
- Maintain the same opportunities and high expectations for *every* pupil in the class.

Within the context of a history lesson, possible solutions for making the subject more accessible for SEN pupils might include the following.

Accessing the material
The role of the teacher is central to the success of any of these strategies. In the first instance, Phillips (2008) emphasizes the importance of effective planning. Does the teacher know who the SEN pupils are in the class? Does he know the nature of the condition and the recommended strategies for overcoming it? If a TA is involved, does she have the scheme of work, lesson plan and textbooks? Has the TA been consulted about the type of activities and resources to use in the lesson?

Cunnah (2000) provides several strategies for tackling the language issue in history lessons. In the first instance, she suggests that teacher talk is kept to a minimum, and is clear and precise. Where pupils have short attention spans, or struggle to decode verbal and non-verbal forms of communication, this is absolutely critical. As Husbands (1996) writes, 'the way teachers talk . . . is of crucial importance to the way pupils learn'. History teachers frequently use abstract terms and concepts, and this can cause tremendous difficulty for some young people. One strategy to alleviate the problem is to provide relevant, interesting examples to illustrate the point being made. In this way, the pupil should have something tangible to relate to the concept being discussed. For example, an explanation of patriotism during the First World War might include reference to battalions of footballers or postal workers formed to encourage recruitment. Having explained the term, and provided an example, teacher should then revisit this material later in the lesson, in order to assess and reinforce understanding.

Encouraging greater use of 'pupil talk' through group work, pair work, role-play or class discussions is an effective way to reduce the amount of teacher talk in the lesson, and to encourage pupils to become more familiar with the language of the subject. Figure 4.1 shows an example of a group exercise which allows pupils to discuss their ideas and to enhance their grasp of historical language. The exercise is entitled 'Elizabethan

---

Elizabethan Speed Dating

Stage 1: Research
- Divide into groups of six.
- Each person will randomly select a character to be during the lesson.
- Read the information about your chosen character.
- The 'Elizabeths' need to form a group and discuss what questions they are going to ask each of the suitors. Focus on the main qualities which would have to be present in a future husband of the Queen.
- The contenders need to discuss the qualities which they need to demonstrate to the Queen.
- Arrange your desks so that each of Elizabeth's suitors is sitting facing her.

Stage 2: The speed date
- 'Elizabeth' has to meet each of her suitors, and ask the same questions to each one.
- She only has 2 minutes to spend with each suitor, before moving on to the next candidate. You will be told when to move onto the next person.
- 'Elizabeth' will have to listen carefully to the responses if she is to reach a verdict on whom, if anyone, she should marry. After each response, she should record her observations on the grid provided.

Stage 3: Group discussion
As a group, discuss the relative strengths and weaknesses of each suitor. Each person in the group should complete their copy of the 'Suitors Grid'. After everyone has completed their grid, come to a group decision on who the best candidate for marrying Elizabeth was. Your list of six options should include the five candidates and 'None of the above: Elizabeth would be better off not marrying'

Figure 4.1 Encouraging 'pupil talk'

Speed Dating', and the lesson objective is to decide who was the most suitable choice of husband for Elizabeth I. As part of the lesson pupils would have to consider a range of criteria such as religion, popular attitudes and foreign policy, thus reinforcing earlier work done on Elizabethan England. Pupils are given a background note, and a brief biography of each contender for Elizabeth's hand in marriage. With a strong emphasis on peer learning and assessment, the exercise supports pupils who may have difficulty reading large chunks of text, or listening to a teacher. In the process, it allows the pupils to articulate and debate their own ideas, whilst giving every pupil the opportunity to succeed.

Reading textbooks and worksheets can also inhibit accessing the subject. Teachers can support learning by providing previously highlighted copies, using a larger font size for their worksheets, and by distributing additional materials as needed, such as glossaries, links to websites, or podcasts. Where possible, provide a greater range of images. These could be augmented by textboxes, or call-outs, so that the text/image is not presented in such a way to deter further enquiry or make the material completely inaccessible.

Perhaps the most important thing a teacher can do is to create and sustain a positive learning environment. Constant encouragement, use of wall displays, support for pupils, and use of a variety of exciting approaches are all necessary to help learners access history. Children need to feel that their work is valued, and that you have very high expectations of them. Most of the research on pupil performance suggests that the biggest contributor to pupil performance is teacher feedback, and experience suggests that this is even more significant when teaching pupils for whom history lessons can be a very challenging environment.

Communicating their historical understanding
The difficulty for SEN pupils is that barriers are erected at two stages in their learning. At the accessing stage they are expected to process content and develop an understanding of the subject. Then they have to communicate this understanding in ways which require a sophisticated grasp of language, structure and historical understanding. The challenge for the teacher is to ensure that pupils do not become frustrated because they cannot demonstrate their understanding of the subject, developed during the accessing stage.

The key to solving this problem is to implement a differentiated strategy. The two main ways of differentiating are by outcome or by task. In the first case, pupils will perform a common open-ended task, and the teacher will differentiate by grading responses at different levels. Differentiating by task involves pupils looking at common topics, but communicating their understanding in a different fashion. Questions may be shorter, require less content, and are therefore more accessible to pupils with learning difficulties. With a structured exercise, questions might get increasingly difficult, thus allowing all pupils the opportunity to demonstrate what they are capable of.

Both approaches have strengths and weaknesses. Whilst differentiation by outcome theoretically allows all pupils to reach the top levels, in reality it can simply reinforce expectations of poor performance, whilst differentiation by task limits opportunities for pupils to demonstrate their full abilities, and frequently results in tasks which have no historical merit at all.

Cunnah (2000) argues strongly for teaching with a wholly inclusive approach at its core, achieved using 'a full range of teaching approaches that allow the opportunity to meet the range of pupil needs'. Differentiation has a place, she argues, but it has to be supported by a belief that 'all children can learn' and a positive learning environment.

In practical terms, this means differentiating in the support provided rather than by the type of task or expectation of pupil performance. At the communication stage, this support can come by allowing pupils to access word-processing facilities, or creating tasks where the response is provided in pictorial form. For some tasks, pupils may be allowed a free choice as to how they present their finished work. In an article for *Teaching History*, entitled 'Does differentiation have to mean different?', Richard Harris (2005) explains why it is necessary, and how it is possible, to motivate pupils and cultivate their curiosity rather than using more primitive methods of teaching lower ability and SEN pupils.

In a landmark pamphlet for the Historical Association, Christine Counsell (1997) stresses the importance of extended writing as a means of performing 'joined up' historical thinking. By completing such a task, pupils will be forced to 'acquire knowledge and to question that knowledge', and, as a consequence, develop their ability to 'empathise and explain'. They will also be able to work towards one of the three historical processes identified in the National Curriculum: to 'present and organise accounts and explanations about the past that are coherent, structured and substantiated, using chronological conventions and historical vocabulary'.

Of course, producing extended writing is difficult for many pupils, particularly those for whom reading, writing, processing and organizing are major issues. Counsell outlines a series of useful ideas for tackling extended writing in an inclusive manner. Central to her work is the need to provide additional guidance and structure for lower ability and SEN pupils. This can come in the form of:

- An organization chart (useful for acquiring information about a topic). This helps the pupil begin to think about selection and relevance of material. Figure 4.2 shows an example.

Did Charles I deserve to be executed?

	Yes	No
Actions before the Civil War		
Responsibility for starting the Civil War		
Role during the Civil War		
Behaviour after the war		
Additional points		

Figure 4.2 Organization chart for considering the issues around the execution of Charles I

- Prompting questions (useful when preparing the answer). Questions such as 'Can you think of an example?' and 'When did this event take place?' can help pupils distinguish between the general and specific, and stress the importance of developing an argument by explaining and illustrating it.
- Writing frame (for the final piece of extended writing). This helps to present the importance of organizing ideas into an analytical structure. You may wish to provide starter sentences for paragraphs, or simply provide suggestions what should be explored in each paragraph. This can even be used for GCSE or A-level students, in order to emphasizing the need to maintain a focus on the question set, to offer a good range of points, and, most importantly, to analyse rather than describe. A partial example where this has been used for an AS essay is provided in Figure 4.3.

How far had conditions for blacks improved in America by 1955?

The most important way that condition for blacks had improved was through the overturning of the 'separate but equal' principle in the 1954 Brown case. This case was important because _____
_____

A further way that conditions for blacks had improved was through the federal recognition of the need to end segregation. This was demonstrated _____
_____

In conclusion, conditions for blacks had partially improved, particularly where _____ was concerned. However, serious problems still remained, with _____ being the most significant. This was so critical because _____
_____

Figure 4.3 Writing frame

From a planning and assessment perspective, these tasks allow the teacher to make relatively straightforward judgements on pupil progression. As a pupil is able to write more confidently, so the teacher can reduce the support provided, and create new challenges for them.

Gifted and talented pupils

◆ *How do we define a 'gifted and talented' pupil?*

In her article written for a *Teaching History* special edition on *Teaching the Most Able*, Deborah Eyre, Director of the National Academy for Gifted and Talented Youth (NAGTY), provided her own definition of gifted and talented. It is a 'term used to describe children or adults who we think have the capacity to achieve high levels of expertise or performance' (Eyre, 2006).

◆ *How do we identify gifted and talented historians?*

There are contested notions concerning how to identify gifted historians. On one level, teachers can use data from assessments, especially where there is some comparability with a national standard, such as GCSE examinations. However, this may exclude certain pupils, who whilst gifted in the subject, are not able to demonstrate their talents in examination conditions. It could also be argued that it would unfairly skew the identification procedure towards pupils who attend well-resourced schools with a strong emphasis on examination performance.

Another, more objective method would be to identify a set of criteria against which young historians could be measured. Here again, there is a problem. Attempts to devise a common set of criteria have provoked considerable disagreement. Haydn et al. (2001) refer to four attempts to categorize able pupils, whilst even government-created bodies struggle to agree, with QCDA, on the one hand, and NAGTY, on the other, disagreeing quite considerably on what makes for an able historian. In 2005, NAGTY convened a history think tank to explore how best to cater for the needs of gifted and talented historians. The report identified the following characteristics of gifted historians (NAGTY, 2005):

- the ability to develop their own 'archive' of knowledge and concepts and the ability to use this to frame and develop questions
- an awareness of the nature of historical interpretation and the ability to historicize representations and constructions of the past, in the light of a range of considerations (such as purpose, provenance, audience, context)
- an understanding of 'presentism' – the inevitable human tendency to see the past in terms of the present – and of the problems and opportunities that this creates
- the ability to cope with the unfamiliar (contexts, periods, cultures) and the ability to use historical imagination to engage with, and attempt to understand, it
- the ability to read actively and critically – to read for purpose and to consider the purposes of the authors and documents that they read
- a willingness to hypothesize, to test and develop ideas and to take risks
- the ability to master, to develop and to experiment with analytical and historical vocabularies and the enjoyment of communicating historical ideas and theories.

However, the QCDA criteria relate much more closely to the attainment targets. So, where the three key processes in the NC are 'historical enquiry', 'using evidence', and 'communicating about the past', the QCDA criteria are grouped under 'literacy', 'historical knowledge', 'historical understanding', and 'enquiry'. Whilst in NC terms there is a certain logic to these criteria, for teachers trying to move a student far beyond the requirements of the NC, they could appear too restrictive. One could also argue that the QCDA criteria do not seem consistent in their ability to stretch very able historians. The ability to 'use subject-specific vocabulary confidently', would not be the preserve of a gifted historian, nor would 'be[ing] intrigued by the similarities and differences between different people's experiences, times and places and other features of the past'. The advantage of the NAGTY criteria, as Phillips (2008) points out, is that they are rooted in definite historical processes, and are therefore specific to the needs of the historian. They also acknowledge that particular historical skills cannot necessarily be broken down into 25 small pieces, as QCDA attempts to do.

◆ How do we meet the needs of gifted and talented historians?

In spite of their disputed criteria, QCDA offers useful general guidance on how teachers can create a learning environment which meets the needs of gifted students. It does not require a huge leap of imagination to see how these could be adapted to serve the purpose of a gifted historian. In their words, the key roles of teachers in this learning environment are to:

- value learners' own interests and learning styles;
- encourage independence and autonomy, and support learners in using their initiative;
- encourage learners to be open to ideas and initiatives presented by others;
- encourage connections across subjects or aspects of the learning programme;
- link learning to wider applications;
- encourage the use of a variety of resources, ideas, methods and tasks;
- involve learners in working in a range of settings and contexts – as individuals, in pairs, in groups, as a class, cross-year, cross-institution and inter-institution;
- encourage learners to reflect on the process of their own learning and to understand the factors that help them to make progress.

(http://www.qcda.gov.uk/2010.aspx)

In order to cover a range of history-specific strategies, I have subdivided the ways to meet the needs of gifted historians into two categories: those which are classroom-based; and those which take place outside the classroom.

In the classroom

For many teachers, under pressure to meet the needs of SEN pupils, conventional learners, those with English as an additional language, as well as those identified as gifted and talented, the easiest way to differentiate is to either tack a couple more questions onto an exercise or to provide some additional reading. There is such tremendous pressure on teachers where inclusion is concerned that it is understandable if the temptation to think 'more equals challenging' prevails. The obvious danger with this strategy, however, is that, as primarily a focus on content, it fails to provide a test of those higher-order skills that the gifted and talented should possess. It also fails to meet the exclusive needs of the gifted student, and can provide just another question to be answered for the speedy student.

NAGTY's approach is to start with the teacher. In order effectively to meet the needs of gifted historians, NAGTY believes teachers must first of all display three qualities:

1. Teachers must be confident in their subject knowledge. This requires a knowledge of how history works, its processes and concepts, as well as the subject matter.
2. Teachers must be risk-takers and innovative.
3. Teachers must be passionate historians, inspirational in the classroom, and able to challenge their students' thinking.

With this in mind, and the suggestions of NAGTY and QCDA, the following list of activities should offer the gifted historian a more challenging classroom experience:

- Test pupils' understanding of the topic by varying how you want it presented. Create tasks which require visual representations of the past, for example a cartoon strip explaining the causes and consequences of Thomas More's quarrel with Henry VIII. In subsequent tasks invite pupils to decide for themselves how they want to present the work. Ask them to explain why they chose that particular medium.
- Using a word-processing package, ask pupils to reorder a passage of narrative so it offers instead a causal analysis of an event.
- Provide opportunities for pupils to devise and pursue their own enquiry questions. For example, introduce the First World War by

presenting a picture of soldiers stuck in mud in Passchendaele. Ask pupils first to place themselves in the picture and suggest the impact which the environment would have had on the different senses of a soldier in that picture. Then ask the class what questions they would want answered to find out more about that scene. After the class have provided their list of questions, in groups, they could distinguish between 'big' and 'small' questions, and in the process, develop their own enquiry to focus on for the First World War.

- Introduce the notion of counterfactual history to pupils. Whilst post-16 pupils may feel comfortable reading the more academic texts on counterfactual history, younger historians will still be challenged by dealing with the 'what ifs' of the period they are studying. Some questions almost write themselves: what if Harold had not been killed at Hastings in 1066? What if Henry VIII had not fallen in love with Ann Boleyn? What if Charles I had won the Civil War? What if Hitler had been killed during the Beer Hall Putsch in 1923?

- The idea of testing understanding through the creation of hypotheticals could be tackled in another way. Ask pupils to create 'conversations in history' between two figures from different periods. One example of this I have used with a set of very able Year 11 pupils was based around a fictional television show called 'After Dark', which hosted an interview between Stalin and Gorbachev, with the purpose of examining in more detail the similarities and differences in their approach to the Cold War, and the different factors that influenced their respective foreign policies. Pupils work in pairs, with each pupil adopting the identity of one of the Soviet leaders. Their initial task was to write a list of questions which they leader would want to ask their counterpart. The eventual discussion not only consolidated their understanding of the origins and conclusion of the Cold War, but also forced the pupils to make links and comparison between the different periods in which Stalin and Gorbachev ruled.

Pupils could also be asked to prepare a treatment for a proposed movie set during the period they are studying. An example of one which I have used with Year 9 pupils looking at the growth of the railways is provided in Figure 4.4. Pupils were given an abridged extract from a newspaper article (Garfield, 2002) which described the opening of the Liverpool–Manchester railway, and a sheet outlining the task.

SMITH PRODUCTIONS

A Greater Manchester Company

We take great pleasure in presenting to you our proposal for a new feature film about the opening of the Liverpool–Manchester Railway.

This event took place on 15 September 1830, and featured many of the important people of the age, all gathered together to witness an occasion marvellous even by the standards of that revolutionary age. The accompanying treatment includes

- A title for the proposed film
- A brief outline of the story (approx. 60 words)
- Description of the principal characters (William Huskisson, Duke of Wellington, fictional bystander? etc.)
- The legacy of this momentous, yet tragic occasion

Figure 4.4 Example movie proposal

Historical simulations can be an effective way to probe pupils' understanding of context and motivation. An obvious topic for such a lesson would be one where a historical figure or group was presented with different options, which would allow the pupils to investigate the possible consequences of each option. President Kennedy's dilemma of how to react to the location of Soviet missiles on Cuba in October 1962 lends itself to this type of task, and is supported by the number of textbooks which outline his options but, critically for the task, do not provide possible consequences. Of course, to make the task more challenging, the pupils could devise the alternative courses of action for themselves.

When using historical sources, do not include the provenance. Invite the pupils to consider when it was produced, and by what type of figure. This forces the pupils to think deeply about the type of language, message, and purpose of the source.

Each of these suggestions places emphasis on open-ended tasks, where pupils have to think beyond and behind the history presented to them. They have to consider why historians have formed their particular judgements, and be able to evaluate them critically. Like the strategies outlined for teaching SEN pupils, these suggestion rely primarily on creating a dynamic learning environment which allows the needs of a particular group of pupils to be met, whilst providing opportunities for the whole.

Beyond the classroom

These activities, in some ways, only create the conditions in which pupils can begin to develop a curiosity for what goes on 'behind the scenes' in history. Understandably, given the need to cater for a wide range of needs, teachers can only offer so much in the context of a normal lesson. However, opportunities to go further with gifted historians present themselves in out-of-class activities. These can be via history societies, debates, extended essays, Oxbridge preparation, old-style Advanced Extension Award questions (which, with their broad focus, can easily be adapted for KS3 and KS4 pupils).

A vital element to meeting the needs of the very able historian is developing their ability to see the links between the history they have studied and the environment around them. This provides two further challenges: to consider what historical sites can tell us about attitudes and beliefs in the past; and to investigate how history is presented to the general public in the modern age.

Teachers therefore need to devise plans to take their history out of the classroom. Chapter 7 provides a detailed look at how teachers can develop the historical interest of pupils outside the classroom, and includes both a wide range of methods and a list of interesting sites for pupils to visit.

Pupils with English as an additional or second language (EAL)

Meeting the needs of pupils whose first language is not English may well be an intimidating prospect for teachers, particularly for those who are just embarking on their career in the classroom. However, with a report in the *Times Educational Supplement* (Roberts, 2005) suggesting that more than 10% of the educational population classified as having EAL needs, it is something that most teachers will have to deal with at some point in their career.

In a subject like history, where comprehension of (sometimes) large amounts of written text and class discussions is necessary before getting down to the serious business of actually 'doing' history, these problems are exacerbated. One of the most challenging lessons in my career began with a Korean pupil arriving unexpectedly in a Year 10 class at the start of the autumn term. She spoke very little English, and had decided to study only scientific subjects for GCSE. She chose history, however, as she believed it would help her improve her understanding of English language. During the course of the next two years, she worked ferociously to master the subject, and achieved a B grade. However, for many EAL pupils, coming to terms with history is not so straightforward, and it is essential that teachers are aware of the different barriers to learning which may exist, and the strategies which can be deployed to overcome them.

◆ *What are the principal barriers to learning for EAL pupils?*

- There may be little prior experience of formal schooling. This means that basic literacy skills, even in their first language, may be lacking.
- Minimal social opportunities within the school where they are in a small minority. Where a pupil is the only person from a particular ethnic or linguistic background, their sense of isolation within the classroom will be increased.
- Little understanding of English language. Where pupils have differing levels of English, teachers also need to diversify their approach to account for any differences which may exist.
- Cultural isolation. The structure of the curriculum may not provide access to content which is either familiar or accessible.
- Diagnosing actual levels of understanding is very difficult when language issues prevent meaningful access to the subject. This subsequently limits the teacher in planning for suitable progression, and may fail to challenge pupils if their individual needs are not being catered for.
- Opportunities to work in pairs or groups, or participate in whole-class discussions, will be severely limited.
- Lack of formal support within the school. Where there is no provision for additional help either inside or outside the classroom from a dedicated assistant, the ability to understand and participate will doubtless be restricted.
- Broader 'settling-in' issues. The ease with which a young person can adapt to a new education system will depend to a large extent on her life beyond their classroom. In addition to the obvious difficulties associated with moving to a new area or country, some children have further problems to contend with, particularly those seeking asylum or for whom there is no support network in place in the local area.

◆ *What strategies can be deployed to make history accessible to EAL pupils?*

The report on *Education for All* (Department of Education and Science, 1985) challenged the prevailing notion that EAL pupils were best served by being withdrawn from mainstream lessons. Instead, it argued that inclusion in lessons, accompanied by appropriate planning and collaboration between teachers and language specialists, would lead to greater progress. The inclusiveness argument has held sway since then, although in recent years many schools have established exclusive induction programmes, which take place outside of lessons, to speed up the process of learning English. However, whichever approach is adopted, the DCSF (2007) stipulate that the priority at all times must be 'to ensure that all young people can achieve their potential, whatever their ethnic or cultural background and whichever school they attend'.

Several sources provide generic advice on how to teach EAL pupils. The QCDA (http://www.qcda.gov.uk/resources/ 5040.aspx), the National Association for Language Development in the Curriculum (NALDIC; see http://www.naldic.org.uk/), the *Times Educational Supplement* (O'Grady, 2000), and most local authorities (see http://www.naldic.org.uk/ITTSEAL2/support/ LEAwebsites.cfm) outline a range of strategies (see also http:// www.ealteacher.com/). A summary of the main points is provided below:

- Allow the use of first languages when the cognitive challenge is likely to be high, or pupils are still developing proficiency in English
- Try to learn a few key words in the first language, such as a greeting, colours, places and the numbers 1–10. This should make the pupil feel more at home in your classroom, and allow you to make a connection to them. Perhaps encourage the class to learn these words too.
- Allow a period of settling-in time, so that the pupil can observe school life in a new country. Perhaps appoint a 'buddy', preferably someone who speaks the same language, to help them during lessons and around the school.
- Use visual images such as photos, diagrams and charts to accompany the work. Link this to key words used in the lesson.
- Seek advice from the SENCO or specialist EAL assistant when planning activities.

- Do not be afraid to correct informal language structures in order to emphasize the structure of language and key phrases.
- Where possible, provide dual-language texts.
- The school should encourage, where possible, active involvement by parents and the local community.

Alongside these measures, history teachers can implement further strategies to develop levels of understanding amongst EAL pupils. The Department for Education and Skills (DfES, 2002) document, *Access and Engagement in History: Teaching Pupils for whom English is an Additional Language*, should be the first point of reference for all teachers encountering EAL pupils for the first time. Whilst sections of the content repeat the generic advice outlined above, the document does provide some useful strategies specific to history:

- When teaching bias, prepare a list of phrases or words which might be used to support a particular viewpoint. Ask the pupils to include as many of the correct phrases as possible. Figure 4.5 provides a brief example of how this might work in practice.

Was Henry VIII a great king?

Write a report giving your view on Henry VIII. The following phrases are provided to help provide bias to your report

Yes	No
Defeated rebels	Executed lots of people
Created Church of England	Selfish and greedy
Took bold decisions	Didn't care who he hurt to achieve his goals
Tried hard to make England a great power	Largely irrelevant to great monarchs of Europe
	Bankrupted the country

Figure 4.5 A list of prompts to examine different points of view

- Make use of ICT where possible. This allows pupils to work at their own speed, and to gain assistance with translation.
- Drama can be an effective medium for developing understanding of written material.
- Use a listening frame and provide a 'buddy' when watching video clips. Provide the pupil with a list of features to look out for, and

specific questions to answer. Allowing them to work in pairs with a 'buddy' should make it easier to follow the clip and to pick out the desired information.

- Deploy directed activities related to text (DART) activities to help develop reading skills, as well as assessing understanding. Examples of such tasks could include sequencing, prioritizing, linking cause and effect, and identifying similarities and differences.
- Provide vocabulary lists for either a series or individual lessons. Ask the pupil(s) to look up the translation in a bilingual dictionary. For example, a lesson examining the origins of the Second World War might include a vocabulary sheet containing the following words: power; dictator; nationalism; fascism; appeasement; remilitarization; communism; democracy; peace; army; arms.
- The teacher could assess the understanding of these terms by providing a list of meanings, and asking the pupil to provide the correct definition or historical term.
- History departments might want to consider how effectively the choice of topics meets the needs of pupils. Is there a case for introducing new topics in order to ease the transition for pupils from diverse ethnic backgrounds?

Tasks

1. Consider opportunities for using role-play with your groups. This is often seen as a time-consuming and historically questionable activity, but it frequently makes the subject appear more accessible for pupils with special educational needs. Try to avoid topics which are naturally exciting, and thus provide an obvious choice for an activity of this kind. Remember, it is those topics that are hardest to make interesting that often provide the greatest challenge to pupils. Think about how you will present the task, and the range of resources which you will present to the pupils. How will they be organized? What guidance will you give them on writing and performing the role-play? How will you assess the task?

2. As a way of challenging gifted and talented pupils, develop an exercise which includes elements of counterfactual history. This could be presented in the form of an adventure game, where the pupil is presented with a series of questions based around historical events, and has alternative courses of action for each one. In this way, the pupil is able to consider the main causes of key historical events, whilst evaluating the larger notion of inevitability in history.

A typical question, therefore, may look something like this.
Issue: Why did the invasion of Normandy in June 1944 succeed?

(i)   You are Rommel, Head of Army Group B. You have at your
       disposal, a whole army in the Pas de Calais. Do you (a) reinforce
       your forces on the Normandy beaches with these troops, or (b)
       keep in them in the Pas de Calais in readiness for the
       anticipated invasion 'proper'?

          If you decided (a) go to question (ii), if you decided (b) go to
       question (iii).

(ii)   Your movement of troops has been hampered by Allied air
       attacks. Only half of the men make it to Normandy without
       suffering injury or death, whilst the Allies have gained a
       foothold around all five landing zones. Do you (a) commit
       these remaining troops into battle immediately, in an attempt
       to drive the Allies back into the sea, or (b) move them to
       defensive positions further east protecting the routes to Paris?

(iii) You appear to have been deceived by the Allies. The troops in
       the Pas de Calais are sitting twiddling their thumbs whilst the
       main invasion gathers momentum in Normandy. Upon
       realizing your mistake, should you keep them where they are or
       move them to protect Paris?

Using ICT to enhance the quality of teaching and learning

5

These days, no self-respecting teacher can claim to be at the cutting edge of teaching and learning without easy access to a computer. Equally, no school wishing to promote itself to prospective parents can do so without highlighting the preponderance of interactive whiteboards, data projectors, wireless laptops and learner response systems scattered throughout the school and used on a daily basis by every child who is fortunate enough to be part of the wonderful cyber-community.

In short, computer technology has progressed from being the once-a-year treat to occupying a central part in the delivery of the school curriculum. This chapter outlines the broader educational benefits of using ICT in the classroom, and provides a variety of practical ways in which it can be used most effectively to enhance the quality of teaching and learning in history.

Why use ICT to enhance teaching and learning?

The strongest argument for using ICT to support existing good practice is that, according to the research, it makes a positive difference to pupil performance. Becta, the government agency responsible for ensuring the most effective use of ICT in education, makes grand claims for the positive effects which technology can have on whole-school performance and the quality of individual learning in particular (Becta, 2008).

The main benefits of using ICT in the classroom can be summarized as follows:

- It provides variety, and therefore allows pupils with different learning styles to feel that their needs are being recognized and catered for. Although the scientific case for the existence of learning styles is unproven, most surveys of pupils suggest that variety of approaches within and across lessons is extremely effective (Younger and Warrington, 2005).
- The interactive nature of ICT-based tasks, twinned with a very visual approach to learning, can help pupils remain motivated and engaged with a task.
- It provides more opportunities for independent learning. Whether conducting web-based research, or downloading an article hosted on a virtual learning environment, computers enable students to carry out extended learning away from the classroom. For those students aiming to go into further or higher education, working in this way helps them develop important research skills required in the next stages of their education.
- It provides opportunities for pair work and peer assessment. Asking pupils to work as 'pilots' and navigators', where one pupil provides the information, and the other inputs it, with only the power to veto an idea, is a great way to ensure pupils understand a task. Providing online forums for pupils to discuss features of a topic creates opportunities for higher-order thinking and peer assessment.
- Investing in ICT is a very clear symbol of a school's commitment to improving levels of pupil performance, and can have a positive impact on pupils' attitudes toward the school.
- Using word-processing packages helps overcome literacy problems, especially when there is a large amount of text already provided. Research for the DfES has also highlighted the advantages of using ICT with pupils with special educational needs (Harrison et al., 2002).
- Technology presents teachers with the ready means to develop cross-curricular links, and to reinforce skills developed in other subject areas. An obvious way for humanities subjects to incorporate numeracy into their teaching is through the use of databases.
- Critically, pupils increasingly prefer to work in this way. Many exploit the potential of ICT in their leisure time, through communications or gaming, and absorb much of their information during a typical day from mobile phones, PDAs or computers. This would therefore suggest that they might find it easier to absorb material in a classroom from similar devices rather than the usual media.
- Using ICT to support learning has been proven to improve pupil performance across the curriculum (Harrison et al., 2002).
- Although not every teacher would welcome it, and there is an

obvious need for prudent behaviour, technology extends support for pupils beyond the classroom, and even beyond the school day. In some schools, it is common practice for pupils to email staff about homework tasks, or for teachers to operate an 'Ask the Expert' online forum, where pupils can post questions about aspects of their course, and receive detailed feedback from the 'expert'.

There are, of course, drawbacks to using ICT. Perhaps the most significant is cost. With laptops costing upwards of £200, projectors around £500, and a class set of learner response pods nearly £2000, any school wanting to exploit the potential of this medium needs to have significant funds at its disposal. The rapidly evolving nature of this technology compounds this problem. There will always be a danger that whatever a school decides to invest in will be out of date by the time most of the staff know how to use it. Some schools attempt to 'futureproof' their ICT investments by constructing five-year plans. Keeping abreast of new technologies through links to local universities is another way to maintain awareness of likely developments. Researchers at Manchester Metropolitan University have established a digital network called CREATE, to enable teachers, lecturers and academics to follow new areas of mutually beneficial areas of research.

This brings us to the issue of staff training. Although most teachers might claim to be proficient in knowing how to use a computer, how many are able to make the most of its potential to develop the quality of learning? A DfES report on the impact of ICT found that where levels of 'e-confidence' were high, there was a positive impact on pupil learning (Prior and Hall, 2004), suggesting that well-trained, proficient staff were an essential factor in making ICT effective as a learning tool. If you want to use ICT effectively in the classroom, you need to get trained up!

A major criticism of technology in classrooms is that it can too easily lead the lesson, rather than support it. Indeed, there is a real danger that a 'computer lesson' is regarded by the pupils as a treat, or a play activity, so that the objective of the lesson becomes 'using the computers'. Again, research suggests that technology enhances learning only when normal good practice is also present (Hattie, 2008). For example, interactive tasks such as producing a video have a significantly greater effect on performance than more passive activities such as web-based research or computer simulations. Overuse of computers at the expense of more traditional methods of teaching can also be detrimental. ICT is but one tool in a teacher's armoury, and ideally should be deployed when it can do things which would otherwise be difficult or impossible to do.

Enhancing the study of history through the use of ICT

If the argument for using technology across the curriculum appears a strong one, can an equally persuasive case be made for history teaching in particular? Ofsted certainly thinks so. Its *History in the Balance* report (Ofsted, 2007) is clear in its view that use of ICT enhances the quality of learning throughout the key stages.

The new National Curriculum for History actually stipulates that all pupils should use ICT from Key Stage 2 'to research information about the past, process historical data, and select, categorise, organise and present their findings'. The programme of study says that this is 'integral to their learning and [will] enhance their engagement with the concepts, processes and content of the subject'. This marks a significant break with the 1990 NC, where the use of ICT was included as only one approach to delivering the subject.

The requirement to use ICT can be explained by four factors:

1. ICT is one of the functional skills included in the NC to prepare pupils for life beyond school. Pupils are therefore expected to 'to find, select and bring together relevant information, develop, interpret and exchange information for a purpose, and apply ICT safely to enhance their learning and the quality of their work'.
2. A recognition that more schools are using technology to deliver history and other subjects (Ofsted, 2000, 2004)
3. Concern about the use of computers by history teachers. Ofsted (2004) indicated that approximately one-third of departments were using them in an unsatisfactory fashion. This view was supported by a DfES report on the impact of new technology on levels of attainment.
4. Although history features prominently amongst subjects using ICT, the difference in grade improvement between schools with high and low levels of use was negligible. (Ofsted, 2004). By requiring teachers to use ICT in specified ways, the NC aims to improve both

the quality of learning and the ways in which the subject is delivered.
5. A belief that using technology creatively leads to more stimulating lessons and improved levels of learning.

This final reason leads us into an exploration of the various ways in which using ICT can enhance the delivery of the key historical processes.

One of the most enjoyable and effective ways in which ICT can enable pupils to investigate and reflect critically on historical questions or issues, is through the use of discussion forums. These enable pupils to discuss features of a topic, using either existing knowledge or as a result of targeted research. Forums offer something different in that they create a framework for debate which can be carried out outside the classroom, and can broaden the range of participants beyond the normal class.

In an early experiment with online forums, the History Department at The Manchester Grammar School invited lecturers from Cambridge University to contribute. Nowadays it can be quite difficult to stop members of the department throwing their two-pennyworth into what are supposed to be pupil discussions! Evidence from my own teaching suggests that pupils tend to write greater quantities, and display stronger signs of higher-order thinking, than they would otherwise do in a similar task carried out on paper. The value of using a forum (see Figure 5.1) over a traditional class debate is that it affords the luxuries of consideration and reflection. Unlike a class debate, pupils have time to construct their submission, and are able to evaluate the quality of previous entries before writing their own. In the process, each contributor will hopefully have any misconceptions about the event corrected, and will be able to add something to the whole class's level of understanding. Martin (2008) suggests that there is a spillover from work done in this fashion into more formal assessment tasks, with a particular benefit to be found in developing both knowledge and understanding, and powers of argument.

A great way to consider notions of relative significance is by constructing a simple graph in a word-processing package, and providing pupils with a list of factors arranged in separate text boxes on the next page. The pupils are thus able to visualize the relative importance of different factors, and, if necessary, make changes to their original work with little fuss. This type of exercise lends itself to ICT as it prevents the need for

> **Tudor Fame Academy: who was the best Tudor monarch 1485–1603?**
>
> In order to reach your decision, consider the state of the kingdom they inherited, the problems they faced, and how they left the kingdom when they died.
>
> Aim to write about 150 words. Who's the best? You decide!!

Figure 5.1 Sample forum exercise

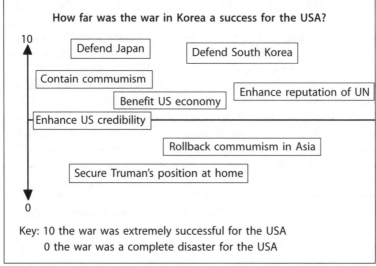

Figure 5.2 Using a word-processor to develop ideas about relative significance

photocopying, cutting, and providing scissors, glue and everything else required to make it work as a paper exercise. Figure 5.2 demonstrates how this was done as a revision exercise for Year 13 students, preparing to sit an A2 module on US foreign policy in Asia.

ICT can help pupils access historical sources via the web, and evaluate them. For example, the Learning Curve provides access to an extensive range of sources covering the major areas of the National Curriculum. Each of the sources is accompanied by questions tailored to the NC Attainment Targets. Examples of these tasks can be found at http://www.learningcurve.gov.uk/snapshots/snapshot39/snapshot39.htm.

An interactive whiteboard can be an invaluable tool when considering visual sources, such as posters or portraits. As they allow pupils to relate directly with the source material, interactive whiteboards provide opportunities for engagement which traditional media do not provide. A teacher might host a painting such as the 'Ditchley portrait' of Queen Elizabeth I by Marcus Gheeraerts the Younger, which we mentioned in Chapter 3, and ask pupils to indicate which aspects of the painting are designed to show off her successes as Queen of England. This task could be performed by the pupils using a photocopied version and pen, but it would lack the impact of a large colour version, and the potential for peer assessment.

In a wide-ranging *Teaching History* article on the challenges of using technology for historians, Ben Walsh (2009) provides a further use of ICT to develop source skills. Focusing on the twin needs to develop source evaluation skills and to treat internet search facilities with caution, he outlines a task where students have to contrast different interpretations of an event found on the internet. The ability to evaluate and cross-reference source material is an essential component of GCSE and A-level history, yet, Walsh argues, many students are satisfied with accepting the perspective of the most popular sites as being authentic. Walsh provides the example of Owen Lattimore, a victim of the McCarthy 'red scare' in 1950s America, to illustrate how the internet can be at best superficial, and at worst downright misleading in its treatment of historical events. A further example, from the same period, is the portrayal of Alger Hiss. Cleared of spying for the USSR in 1949, but convicted of perjury a year later, after evidence came to light which suggested he had, in fact, acted as a Soviet agent since the 1930s, the question of Hiss's guilt remains a divisive issue. Anyone coming to the topic fresh, hoping for a nice, accurate summary of the case, might do well to avoid the internet altogether. However, as the focus of an exercise evaluating reliability or utility it is extremely productive.

Increasingly, pupils choose to present more in-depth explanations about the past on word-processors. It is rare occurrence indeed when one of my Year 12 and 13 students submits a handwritten essay. The advantages for the student of constructing an answer in this way are numerous. Firstly, it offers the potential for easy editing, possibly after a draft has been emailed to the teacher. Second, using the spell check facility can prevent *some* careless errors undermining the overall impression of the essay. Third, where a student is using a writing frame, use of textboxes can provide a guide for how much needs to be written. Finally, it often makes the work look more professional, betraying a sense of pride in a job well done.

ICT allows pupils to communicate their knowledge and understanding of history effectively. Relating back to Ofsted's desire for history in schools to reflect how it is presented and accessed by the wider public, many departments host their own departmental website, or contribute to whole-school sites. The purpose of this is to publicize the work of the department and to support the learning of the pupils. In some cases, pupils will themselves establish their own websites or blogs devoted to their study of history.

ICT can also help develop the skills required to communicate effectively. A commonly used method is through pupil-delivered PowerPoint presentations, but increasingly webcasts and podcasts are being used to provide a more exciting form of presentation. Once again, technology's ability to offer opportunities to review material, and to provide a visual prompt or stimulus, ensures that it can offer a unique approach to historical study.

Using software packages to enhance teaching of history

As indicated above, ICT offers a multitude of ways to enhance the quality of teaching and learning in history. The purpose of this section is to illustrate how the most accessible and manageable software programmes can be used in the classroom.

◆ *Word-processors*

In a survey of ICT use by history teachers, Haydn (2002) found that, after TV, video and the internet, word-processing was the most popular form of ICT activity. Several factors contribute to its popularity. Perhaps most importantly for teachers, it is both accessible and easy to use. It is also very flexible and can be used for presentational purposes as well as for a task. Material created in a document is relatively straightforward to amend and can be adapted to make it easier or more challenging.

It is also a highly effective tool. In the same survey, the teachers who were interviewed stated that the word-processor was the most helpful form of ICT for teaching history. This reinforces an oft-quoted verdict of Ben Walsh (1998: 6) on the power of the word processor:

> It can search, annotate, organise, classify, draft, reorganise, redraft and save that fundamental of the historian, the printed word. When we consider these processes, and the implicit difficulties they represent for so many of our pupils, the true power and value of the word processor becomes clear. It is not a typewriter, it is an awesome tool for handling information.

In the following we outline a number of practical uses of word-processors to enhance the quality of lessons.

Source evaluation

Presented with a single source, pupils can use the highlight or comment tools to identify aspects of the source which suggest that it is not an entirely trustworthy piece of evidence. Text boxes could also be used to perform the same function, especially where a visual source is used.

They can also use the same tool to identify areas of similarity and difference between sources. Cross-referencing is an important historical skill, and is assessed at GCSE and A level. Some pupils rely on rewriting the sources, rather than making firm comparisons. Using the ICT in this way could help.

Causation

After pupils have completed some research on a topic, or even as a means of assessing understanding after completing the topic, they could complete an exercise such as the one in Figure 5.3. The first part of the exercise, testing pupils' knowledge of the course content, offers a list of explanations for the outbreak of the English Civil War, mixed up with a smaller number of red herrings. After reviewing their previous work, the pupils need to decide which explanations are correct, and delete those that are incorrect. This works most effectively when pupils act in pairs, with one taking the role of 'pilot', and the other as 'navigator'. The navigator is the only one able to make suggestions, and the all the pilot can do is work the machine and veto what he believe is a wrong answer. This encourages co-operative working and peer assessment.

The decision-making process then became more challenging, as the pupils are presented with the task of identifying similarities between the factors, and deciding which type of

THE CAUSES OF THE ENGLISH CIVIL WAR

1. Remove any statement which you believe is not a major cause of the Civil War

   ☐ People were unhappy with religious changes introduced under Charles

   ☐ Parliament annoyed Charles at the start of his reign by refusing to grant him customs duties

   ☐ Parliament wanted to replace Charles as king with a foreign prince

   ☐ Charles didn't want Parliament to control the Army

   ☐ Charles wanted to abolish Parliament

   ☐ Charles married a Catholic who wanted to convert the whole of England

   ☐ Charles refused to make ship money illegal

   ☐ Parliament feared that Charles was planning to bring Catholics from Ireland to crush Protestants in England

   ☐ The future of the bishops lead to divisions amongst Members of Parliament

   ☐ Charles' belief in divine right clashed with Parliament's belief in its own importance

   ☐ The power of Parliament had steadily grown since the English Reformation

   ☐ Parliament objected to many of Charles' advisers

   ☐ The Nineteen Propositions forced the King and his supporters to take action against Parliament

   ☐ Ship money and coat and conduct money led to a taxpayer's strike

2. Drag and drop each remaining cause into the correct box. If necessary, you can amend the size of each box as appropriate.

ECONOMIC FACTORS *(concerned with financial matters)*	POLITICAL FACTORS *(concerned with how decisions are made and where power lies)*	SOCIAL FACTORS *(concerned with living standards and lifestyles)*

3. Write a paragraph, in the space below, explaining which factor you believe was the most important in causing the English Civil War. To help you make your decision, you may wish to consider which factor is linked to several others. Use **Times New Roman**, font size **12**.

Figure 5.3 Identifying causation

cause each factor represents. They then have to drag each factor into one of three textboxes labelled 'Political factors', 'Economic factors' and 'Social factors'.

After this second stage of the activity has been completed, the pupils have to type a short conclusion which identifies the most important type of cause for the English Civil War.

Organize ideas and evidence

Word-processors allow pupils to identify essential information in large pieces of text, which they can then group or categorize, or drag into a table (see Figure 5.4). The facility to drag text around within a table allows a teacher to create exercises which test understanding, whilst helping the pupil to develop their extended writing skills (see Figure 5.5).

What was King James really like?

Source A   Sir Anthony Weldon (1650)
He was so crafty and cunning in petty things … as a very wise man was wont to say he believed him the wisest fool in Christendom, meaning him wise in small in things but a fool in weightier affairs.

Source B   Sanders (1650)
King James, whose wisdom in his sovereignty had esteem beyond any contemporary.

Source C   Report on England by the Venetian Ambassador (1607)
He is sufficiently tall, of a noble presence, his physical constitution robust, and he is at pains to preserve it by taking much exercise at the chase, which he passionately loves, and uses not only as recreation, but as a medicine. He is Sovereign in name and appearance rather than in substance and effect.

How far do the sources suggest that James I was a good king?

Hint: copy phrases from each source into the table under the correct heading. After you have done this, try and group together phrases which make similar points about James I.

Positive view of James I	Negative view of James I

Figure 5.4 Using a word-processor to compare evidence

FEATURE OF COLD WAR TENSION	HOW IT WAS REMOVED FROM THE COLD WAR?	EVIDENCE
Ideology	Barriers between East and West Berlin were removed/ East and West agreed on a post-war settlement for Germany	
The Arms Race	The USSR reduced its commitments outside the Soviet Bloc	
Soviet control of Eastern Europe	The USA and USSR agreed to reduce their nuclear arsenals	
Extension of the Cold War to the Third World	The USSR embraced Western political and economic values/The home of communism disappeared	
Control of Germany	Communist governments in Eastern Europe were overthrown, and the USSR did not interfere	

HOW DID THE COLD WAR COME TO AN END?
By rearranging the information in the second column, and selecting the appropriate evidence from the timeline in your books, complete the table so it correctly explains how the Cold War came to an end.

Figure 5.5 Using a word-processor to organize ideas and evidence

Revelatory writing

Prior and John (2000) argued that the potential to develop historical skills using word-processors was not fully recognized by teachers. Even if they used some of the techniques outlined above, they felt that pupils could, through guesswork or the process of elimination, perform the tasks without the need for any great historical ability. Building on their work at Bristol University, they developed a process of 'revelatory writing' which is used to augment rather than copying text.

The essence of the exercise involves three stages:

1. Researching key features of a period or individual's life.

2. Discussing a bland account of the same period/ individual, and suggesting how to improve it.
3. Adding material to the bland account, making use of factual details, assertions, anecdotes, interpretations. Pupils could also be encouraged to transform the original text into something which articulates a particular viewpoint.

According to Prior and John, this approach forces pupils to use historical skills such as source evaluation, knowledge and understanding, organization and selection in order to complete the task. It also has the additional advantages of being suitable for all ability levels, and can be easily amended to work with audio or video material.

◆ *PowerPoint*

PowerPoint, like word-processors, is a very flexible piece of software. Not only is it a tremendous device for pupil presentation, it also provides opportunities for innovative teaching to take place. Most teachers will use presentation software to either display images or provide a structure to a formal lecture-style lesson. However, even these otherwise traditional approaches can be enlivened with only a small amount of creativity. Visual images could be presented with attention drawn to particular features, whilst lecture slides could feature embedded video clips, downloaded from sites such as www.britishpathe.com.

When building a PowerPoint presentation, it is important to remember that, where content is concerned, less is more. The slides should only highlight key points, and should never simply reproduce what you are saying. Ensure that there is a clear structure to your presentation; use headings and key questions to guide your audience. Remember that variety is as important in a presentation as it is in a lesson. Try and include hyperlinks, audio/video clips or discussion questions.

This type of software is also a tremendously exciting tool to use with pupils. Some suggestions for using PowerPoint as a more pupil-centred activity include the following:

- Present them with a source surrounded by text boxes. The pupils have to place the source in context by explaining features of the source linked to by each text box. This activity can also be used to identify evidence of subjectivity in a source.
- Pupils can create their own work. This develops research skills, as

well their ability to select, organize and communicate. When presented to their peers, it can also lead to a useful peer exercise. Teachers can ask pupils to create the presentation in different formats, such as a mind map or including audiovisual or web links.

Alternatives to conventional presentation packages are increasingly available online. Web-hosted packages, such as www.prezi.com allow users to store and present information in innovative ways, and bring more variety to slide shows.

◆ Databases

Whilst databases may not appear to be the most attractive or sophisticated of tools, as far as developing historical skills is concerned, they are arguably the most useful. They allow pupils to identify trends over time, to investigate hypotheses, and to build up a detailed picture of events, without the need to consult a large amount of text. At a more advanced level, they invite pupils to establish their own hypotheses, and to question the utility of the data itself. They even empower pupils to construct their own evidence by building up a database of their own from scratch.

Databases lend themselves to almost any kind of historical enquiry, and can be quite straightforward to construct. One example is provided by Nicola Goodwin, a PGCE student at MMU, who developed a database of First World War casualties who had attended The Manchester Grammar School whilst on placement there (Figure 5.6). Nicola then produced a worksheet to accompany the database, a section of which is included in Figure 5.7.

Other public sources of data can be found in public libraries, and of course, on web-based portals such as ancestry.co.uk, which provides access to censuses, parish records, court records, details of immigration and emigration, and a huge range of other collections.

Original source material from the Prestwich Asylum archives held by Greater Manchester County Record Office has also been converted into a spreadsheet, to enable pupils to trace the history and development of mental healthcare and examine changing attitudes and values towards the mentally ill. This can be found at http://www.gmcro.co.uk/education/education4.htm, with teacher materials available to accompany the data set.

Surname	First Name(s)	Position	Unit	How he died	Day of death	Month of death	Year of death	Where he died	Age at death	When at school
Ackroyd	Charles Winstanley	Private	44th Australian Contingent	Killed in action		October	1917	Menin Road, nr Ypres	23	1908–11
Alcock	George	Private	20th (S.) Bn. R.F.	Taken prisoner	31st	July	1916	Vélu		1904–07
Allen	Frank Ernest	Private	1/6th Bn. Manchester Regiment	Killed in action	27th	May	1915	Dardanelles	20	1908–10
Allured	Will	Second Lieutenant	6th Border Regiment	Killed in action	14th	September	1916	France	22	1905–08
Almond	William Edmondson	Corporal	R.G.A.	Killed in action	Born in 1889					1904–06
Armstrong	William Kingo	Captain	1/4th Bn. South Lancs. Regiment	Killed in action	11th	April	1918		26	1905–07

Figure 5.6 Extract from Old Mancunians First World War database

This database contains information about 186 former MGS boys who died in the First World War. You will be using the 'sort' and 'filter' tools to find as much information as you can.

1. You are first going to use the 'Filter' tool to identify a particular individual.
   - This soldier died in 1917
   - He was 23 when he died
   - He was 'killed in action'
   - He was a private

   Write his name here:

   Write three other facts you can learn about him from the database:

   His name can be found in two places in the school, can you think where?

2. The Average Soldier
   Using the database, we are going to create an 'average soldier'.

   (a) Use the 'Sort' tool to put surnames into alphabetical order to work out which was the most common. Choose one of the most common names.
   (b) Do the same for first names.
       The name of your average soldier is:
       Are the names very different to the names you have in your class today?
   (c) How old was the average soldier when they died? (*Boys could also be asked to produce a graph*)
       Use the 'Sort' tool to find the most common age and enter your answer here:
   (d) In what year did the average soldier die?
   (e) Where did the average soldier die?
       Use the 'Filter' tool to find out what major battles took place where soldiers died in 1916. Choose one of these battles and do some research to discover some extra information about it. Write this below.

       Battle Information:

3. Filling in the gaps
   Charles Fry was a teacher at the school. There is a memorial for him near the Main Stairwell. Find his record.

There are some gaps in his record. See if you can find out how old he was when he died, where he is buried, and what R.F.A. stands for. Use this website: http://www.cwgc.org/debt_of_honour. asp?menuid=14

If you have time, see if you can fill in the gaps for any other records using the same website.

Figure 5.7 Sample activities for using a database

◆ *Digital video*

A combination of cheaper hardware and the proliferation of web-based video clips has prompted a revolution in home video recording and, in particular, home-based video editing. Inevitably, these techniques have found their way into the classroom, and provided another way in which new technologies can be used to enhance learning.

Digital video can function as both an authoring and an evaluative tool. Used as an authoring tool, pupils can produce a commentary to be read over the top of existing footage. In this way it acts as an alternative to producing a traditional piece of extended writing. Pushing this task a stage further, pupils could be given a collection of clips and be required to produce their own documentary, deciding which clips to use, which to omit, and what order to arrange them. Once the visual aspect of the task has been completed, the new commentary can then be narrated over the top.

Requiring pupils to work with digital video tests their ability to select, organize, and prioritize. It also involves a large amount of peer review, and therefore is a useful AfL task. It can also be used to develop source evaluation and interpretation skills. Building on the idea behind 'revelatory writing', you could ask pupils to create their own interpretations, for example a British propaganda film from the Second World War. One of the great features of editing your own film is that you can change the structure of existing films, and splice footage from documentaries to create something entirely new.

One idea for using digital video to study local history is to interview members of the local community, perhaps former pupils of the school. If you're lucky enough to have contacts with pupils from the 1930s and 1940s, pupils could produce their own film about the impact of the war on the school. Smith (2008) provides an example of how this was done for an extended research task.

There are a large number of sites which allow free clips to be downloaded. Some of the best include:

http://www.learningcurve.gov.uk/focuson/film/
Focus On Film is a jointly funded project by The National Archives and the South East Grid for Learning. This site presents film as a historical source and considers its advantages and disadvantages as evidence for the past.

http://www.timelines.tv/#
Free online resource based on documentaries written, produced and presented by the award-winning Andrew Chater.

http://www.open2.net/creativearchive/index.html
Open University site with an extensive range of clips.

http://www.bfi.org.uk/creativearchive/titles/
An esoteric collection of films, consisting of early documentaries, silent comedies, literary adaptations and transport films.

http://www.itnsource.com/
Large number of news clips, and silent footage from the archives of Independent Television News (ITN).

http://www.channel4.com/4od/whatson/index.html
Provides free access to library of Channel 4 programmes, and allows users to buy content from National Geographic and Discovery channels.

http://www.archive.org/details/prelinger
Contains thousands of 'ephemeral films', covering education, advertising, industry, and amateur footage. Includes some great examples of Cold War propaganda!

http://www.pbs.org/history/
US-based Public Broadcasting Service homepage. Features downloadable clips and other resources from most of their documentaries.

Whilst the prospect of filming, editing and narrating a short film can appear daunting, in reality the process is very straightforward. A number of teachers are already making use of small handheld digital recorders, such as the Flip, which are cheap, easy to use and plug directly into a computer's USB port. Once the clips are uploaded, these can be edited using a package such as Movie Maker, which comes free with most versions of Windows. This uses the same principles as a Word document, as material can be dragged and dropped into a storyboard, and a soundtrack or commentary imported from the hard drive, or recorded 'live' over the footage.

◆ *Learner response pods*

One of the newest developments in the use of ICT in the classroom is the introduction of individual voting systems or voting response pods into teaching. Whilst there are different versions of these on the market, the principle behind them is the same. In essence, after a teacher has either asked a question, or displayed one on the screen, each pupil enters their response on their pod. The responses are sent directly to a hub, and quickly appear on the screen. Most systems now allow users to enter text as well as numbers, thus enhancing quite considerably the range of potential uses for the devices.

The benefits of using learner response systems include the following:

- By providing every pupil, or pairs, with a 'pod' teachers are able to obtain a response from everyone in the class, not just those who choose to put their hand up.
- Experience suggests that they are tremendously motivating for pupils, especially when used for 'starter' activities.
- As well as being useful for recalling factual information – dates, names, etc. – they can also be used for higher-order thinking. By using the rank-order facility, pupils can learn to analyse and evaluate relative significance.

Using the pods does not replace pupil talk, it actually increases both its volume and quality, as more pupils will be comfortable about contributing if they can see their ideas area already informing the learning which is taking place in the classroom, and their discussions will become more reflective rather than summative.

- Laffin (2009) outlines how voting systems can be used to enhance role-play activities, which themselves often lead to excellent learning outcomes. Laffin used the pods to assess the differing reactions to government policy in the first part of Henry VIII's reign. Her research suggested that good preparation was essential if the exercise is to work well, which would be the case for any sixth-form discussion or role-play. However, she also found that the pods were 'versatile, exciting and appealing'. The pupil response was also positive, with the visual and inclusive nature of the systems proving to be especially important.

- The pods provide immediate feedback to teachers on levels of understanding part way through a task. If a teacher wanted to assess how many pupils had a problem with a (conventional) task during the lesson, he could ask them to indicate via their pods. As the pods can be either named, or used anonymously, this should not lead to too much embarrassment being felt by any pupil who did not understand the material. Once again, here is an example of new technologies performing a useful AfL role.

◆ *Virtual Learning Environments (VLEs)*

VLEs may already be familiar to you, as most university PGCE departments use them to share information and encourage discussion about aspects of teaching. VLEs can be used to build up a discreet learning community, which can access, interact with and contribute to an online course both at school and at home. The broad functionality of VLEs means that the teacher can use them in many different ways to enhance learning. Most VLEs usually include the potential to

- create discussion forums;
- host quizzes;
- mark and grade online;
- create surveys;
- upload documents;
- upload links to websites;
- create blogs and wikis;
- host message boards;
- create databases.

In schools, the most common approach is to create courses for departments, which then develop separate pages for each year group or module. An example from part of a course created for an A2 unit on the US in Korea and Vietnam is provided in Figure 5.8.

VLEs therefore provide teachers with the ability to create entire courses, either for particular topics, or to run alongside the normal teaching schedule. In doing so, they can stimulate additional research with uploaded materials or web links, create online seminars using the discussion board, provide material for

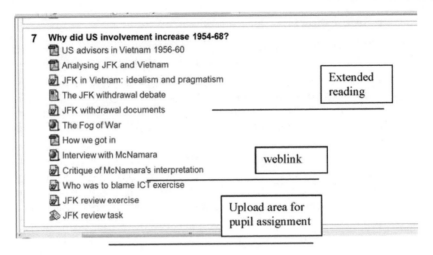

Figure 5.8 Extract from a VLE course

pupils who may have missed lessons, and allow time for reflection and review. Snape and Allen (2009) describe one scenario where a VLE was used to create an 'e-book' to support pupils studying the Crusades. The concept of the 'e-book' is useful for teachers who wish to develop a standalone series of lessons and out-of-class activities on a particular topic. In this case, Snape and Allen uploaded various types of materials and activities, which would eventually feed into discussion forums embedded in each 'chapter' of the 'e-book'. Approaching the topic in this way highlighted the power of VLEs to facilitate differentiation and personalized learning, whilst providing a secure narrative context for all pupils. Participating in the forums also made a positive impact on pupils' ability to argue, consider hierarchy and to challenge historical interpretations. Phillips (2008) warns of the dangers inherent in using VLEs to dump course content without attention to presentation or structure. The beauty of Snape and Allen's model is that it ensures that the VLE is used constructively to display resources and to direct learning. Like any collection of resources, the VLE will be most effective when prior thought has gone into how it will appear to the intended audience.

◆ *Mini-blogs*

If you really want to embrace emergent technologies to develop your teaching, consider the educational uses of websites such as www.blogger.com, which can be used to host course materials and information updates to users, or www.edmodo.com, which works in a similar way to a social networking site, but is designed specifically for educational uses. One way in which I have used this site is to support Year 13 students doing A-level coursework. I can maintain contact with the set, reminding them of deadlines, providing new links to useful websites, and create discussions and polls. They can also keep in touch with the research being done by others in the group. As a result, we can create the feel of a genuine 'research community', allowing for the sharing of ideas, and preparing them in a different way for the next stage in their educational careers.

Finally, I can strongly recommend the website http://www.boxoftricks.net/ – an amazing compendium of web links and ideas for using ICT in new and exciting ways.

Tasks

1. ICT audit

   It is a good idea to periodically review your ability to use ICT to support learning. By completing this simple audit, or even one you have developed yourself, you can identify areas to target in future.

Area of competence	On a scale of 1–10, how familiar am I with it? (1=not at all, 10=extremely)	On a scale of 1–10, how confident am I that I can use it to enhance teaching and learning?
Word-processing		
PowerPoint		
Digital video		
Databases		

Area of competence	On a scale of 1–10, how familiar am I with it? (1=not at all, 10=extremely)	On a scale of 1–10, how confident am I that I can use it to enhance teaching and learning?
Individual devices, e.g. learner response systems/pods		
VLE		
Imaging software, e.g. Paint/ Photoshop		
Podcasts		
Desktop publishing		
The internet		

2. Design a website evaluation exercise

   The National Curriculum requires pupils to 'identify, select and use a range of historical sources, including textual, visual and oral sources, artefacts and the historic environment, and to evaluate the sources used in order to reach reasoned conclusions'.

   With this in mind, design an exercise which aims to look at the reputation of of a particular historical figure or event. As part of the exercise, pupils have to select two websites which present contrasting interpretations of the individual or event. They could then carry out a series of investigations where the sources were evaluated and compared. Can they find examples of factual errors? Is there evidence of exaggeration in the language? Can they find out anything about the provenance of the website? After comparing the two websites,-pupils could decide which would be the most useful to a historian.

Teaching emotive and controversial issues in history

A controversial historical issue is one in which there are competing values and interests, where there is a likelihood that emotions become strongly aroused, and around which there may be tremendous political or cultural sensitivity. Almost any topic can become controversial if individual groups offer differing explanations about events, what should happen next and how issues should be resolved, or if one side of an issue is presented in a way that provokes an emotional response in those who might disagree.

The nature of the controversy may be in a disputed version of what has happened or why something happened in the past. It may also be the case that a narrative reaching to the present day is involved, with emotive responses to the case of current situations, and desirable ends to work towards.

It is therefore self-evident that these issues are frequently complex, and require the teacher to be knowledgeable, fair, impartial and sensitive in order to ensure desirable learning ends are met.

Why should I teach controversial issues?

1. The issues are in the curriculum. The National Curriculum requires pupils to know and understand major events, changes and developments in British, European and world history. This includes coverage of issues such as colonization, immigration, genocide, and nationalism.

2. It will help pupils make links to other periods of history which they have studied.

   Analogy is an extremely useful tool for historians, as it allows us to place events into some kind of context. By comparing an event to something similar in another country or in another period, historians are able to gain a clearer sense of scale and significance.

3. Pupils find these issues interesting. For many young people, learning about emotive issues humanizes the subject. It allows them to make a connection between their own experiences and those of people from the past. In the process, it allows pupils to respond to the past in an emotional as well as intellectual fashion.

4. Young people want to know more about global issues. Exploring the origins of controversial issues and attempts to resolve them allows pupils to make links with contemporary issues, and the work of organizations such as the United Nations, European Union, and non-governmental organizations. Indeed, the NC says that pupils should be 'encouraged to make links with issues of the present day'. It also provides a natural overlap with much of the citizenship curriculum.

5. Controversial issues can help develop thinking skills. A key aim of the new secondary curriculum is to develop those skills required to succeed in school and beyond. Studying history, as a subject in its own right, can help young people acquire many of these personal, learning, and thinking skills, and the study of emotive and controversial issues is especially useful for making young people become reflective, creative, effective and independent individuals.

As Kinloch et al, (2005) emphasize, history is primarily concerned with questions; therefore studying these types of issues provides plenty of opportunities to interpret and evaluate competing views on the past.

What factors might constrain the teaching of controversial issues in history?

The TEACH report (Historical Association, 2007) identifies eight constraints which apply to all key stages, and offers several more which are specifically applicable to KS3 upwards.

1. The amount of time given to history in the curriculum
   The issue. It is no secret that the place of history in the curriculum is

under threat. A combination of factors has led to a significant fall in the number of young people studying the subject. A request by the Conservative Party under the terms of the Freedom of Information Act found that two-thirds of GCSE students did not take history in 2008. This figure was also down on the 1997 figure by almost 3½%. The introduction of diplomas in 2008 is likely to place an additional squeeze on the numbers of pupils studying history. Simply put, if fewer pupils are choosing to study the subject, there are fewer opportunities to teach these issues.

The solution. Obviously, there is no magic solution beyond continuing to explain to curriculum managers why history is important, and ensuring that your exciting and stimulating lessons make history a subject that young people want to study at GCSE and beyond.

2. Playing it safe

   The issue. Pressure to meet the demands of external examination board syllabuses and to cover as much of the QCDA schemes of work as possible can lead to schools 'glossing over' emotive issues in their push to finish the course.

   The solution. Consider ways in which controversial issues could be given greater emphasis. When planning the teaching of a topic, you could place the issue at the heart of the course, emphasizing its importance to the period.

3. Training

   The issue. Few history teachers will be given the opportunity to access high-quality training on teaching emotive and controversial issues. Reductions in CPD budgets have meant greater emphasis has been placed on providing training 'in-house', and when teachers are allowed to attend external CPD training, it is frequently related to KS4 or KS5 delivery.

   The solution. As a department, you could devote a series of departmental meetings to discussing how to deliver a course such as this, using the time to outline potential pitfalls, lesson plans and resources. You could extend this process by involving members of other departments who also teach controversial issues. Depending on the level of interest, it could form the basis of an 'action research' programme for a small number of interested staff.

4. Availability of quality resources

   The issue. One of the central themes of the TEACH report is the link between well-informed, confident practitioners and effective teaching. Clearly, the lack of adequate training is one factor undermining the development of an appropriately informed workforce, but the relative lack of specialist materials also mitigates against the teaching of emotive issues. Most resources on the market are pitched at specific periods of history or produced for particular topics within the scheme of work.

The solution. There is plenty of evidence to suggest that the most effective resources are those produced either by the teacher or by pupils themselves. You could work with a colleague to develop resources for the teaching of a controversial issue, and exploit the many ideas for teaching these topics provided in journals such as *Teaching History*. Issue 120 is devoted to the topic of teaching controversial issues, and includes man useful practical examples.

5. Inadequate teacher subject knowledge

The issue. Lack of security of knowledge can often lead to poor learning and a tendency to treat all topics in a similar way, thus denying pupils the opportunity to tackle controversial issues in a way that brings out the range of issues and allows scope for meaningful debate. Where the subject is taught by a non-specialist, the issue of poor subject knowledge is even more problematic. As Kinloch (2005) writes, the rush to integrate a study of the Muslim world into the curriculum after 9/11 potentially created a further problem by suggesting that Islam and the West were separate and hostile entities.

The solution. The only way that this problem will be solved is through teacher research. Where a non-specialist is timetabled to deliver the lessons, the history department needs to help the teacher become more familiar with the issues and the period as a whole

6. Deliberate avoidance of controversial topics

The issue. The TEACH report famously stoked a huge controversy when it claimed that a small number of schools had chosen not to teach the Holocaust for fear of offending Muslim children. It cited other examples where topics such as the slave trade, the Arab–Israeli conflict and the Crusades were deliberately avoided in order to prevent teachers causing offence to pupils and parents. A chain email, which appeared shortly after the publication of the report, erroneously claimed that Holocaust teaching was banned in the UK, prompting Alan Johnson, the then Secretary of State for Education and Skills to state in 2007 'that there are certain subjects which will be protected in the new curriculum and that includes the Holocaust'.

Fear of causing offence to a particular party is only one reason why teachers may choose to avoid teaching a topic. As previously stated, lack of adequate knowledge could also play a part, as could a feeling the material was not appropriate for certain age groups. A teacher may also argue that, with the development of a formal citizenship curriculum, these types of issues are best being dealt with through that subject, rather than in a history lesson.

The solution. Teachers need to remember that the value of teaching emotive and controversial issues in history often outweighs any potential risks.

7. Lack of balance

The issue. In order for pupils to gain a full understanding of the past, it is essential that teachers do not seek to present the actions and attitudes of differing groups in a one-dimensional manner. For example, not all white men were willing participants in the slave trade, and not every black slave was a powerless figure. Teachers need to consider how their portrayal of different groups will impact upon pupils who are members of the same race, ethnic group, or religion.

The solution. This comes back to the need to prepare and plan thoroughly. A teacher does not want to be in a position where the pupils feel embarrassed or even resentful as a result of the approach being taken. It is therefore important to recognize and identify the differing attitudes and actions which existed within different communities as well as between them. A teacher should also try and avoid portraying people in the past as being inferior or stupid, and instead encourage pupils to examine carefully the context in which people lived.

8. Can pupils ever really understand emotive events if they were not there?

The issue. The Holocaust Memorial Museum in Washington, DC, has been criticized by some Holocaust survivors as just a large collection of photographs (Phillips, 2008). Without the complete experience – the sounds, smells and fear of the camps – no museum could ever present a truly accurate representation of the Holocaust. This argument can be broadened to encompass any exhibition on a historical issue, whether it be the slavery gallery at Liverpool's Maritime Museum or the reconstruction of a cotton mill at Styal in Cheshire. The problem, therefore, is that if a pupil cannot get a deep understanding of an issue, perhaps this issue should not be taught at all.

The solution. All historians have to rely on a degree of historical imagination when constructing their versions of the past, and the same is true for pupils studying the subject. Although, if done badly, this can lead to the practice of a form of historical guesswork or superficial judgements being made, empathy is a powerful device for bringing the past to life for pupils.

Teachers can use various means to encourage an empathetic approach. They can create role-play exercises, use an array of primary source material, and even use out-of-school visits.

How should I teach emotive and controversial issues?

◆ Keep pupils focused on the history

Whilst there will be obvious links to other subjects, and, indeed, to the home experiences of some pupils, it is important for pupils to retain a clear historical focus. Although the approach may differ for teaching an emotive or controversial issue, the same historical processes need to be followed if the quality of enquiry is to be assured.

To this end:

- encourage pupils to base their statements on evidence, rather than conjecture or prejudice
- emphasize that it is not important to adopt a fixed position on an issue. Allow them to feel comfortable in not having to make a clear judgement
- cultivate an inquisitive approach to all aspects of the issue. Remind the pupils that the source analysis skills which they would use on other sources are even more critical when considering sensitive historical issues

◆ Cut out classroom incivilities

Research by Boice (1996) identified the most common forms of teacher or pupil behaviour that impacted on pupil performance. The main forms of teacher incivility include dismissive remarks, not taking pupils or their ideas seriously, and adopting teaching styles that do not meet the needs of the learners.

The most common examples of pupil incivility include poor behaviour, lack of preparation, lateness, and distracting other pupils. Failure to eradicate these can create a learning environment where pupils do not feel the topic is worth taking seriously, or are not comfortable expressing themselves.

In order to establish a more 'civil' classroom environment, the following action should be taken:

- Lay down your ground rules right from the start. Let the class know what you expect of them in terms of attendance, punctuality and conduct. An Oxfam (2006) paper on teaching controversial issues provides a useful overview of what to expect from pupils:

  ✓ Only one person to talk at a time – no interrupting.
  ✓ Show respect for the views of others.
  ✓ Challenge the ideas, not the people.
  ✓ Use appropriate language – no racist or sexist comments.
  ✓ Allow everyone to express their views to ensure that everyone is heard and respected.
  ✓ Pupils should give reasons why they have a particular view.

- Adopt a positive behaviour management strategy. If there are signs that behaviour is deteriorating, investigate why. Are the pupils bored? Are they able to see the relevance of the topic?
- Avoid judging responses; instead offer positive feedback.
- Use non-verbal as well as verbal means of communication. Smile, be expressive in response to pupils' points and questions.

◆ *Encourage an open-minded approach*

Pupils with very fixed ideas on an issue may struggle to see a problem in a way other than 'black and white'. However, one of the main reasons for studying controversial issues is to develop pupils' thinking skills and to recognize that people may interpret an event or issue in different ways. It is therefore necessary to move pupils from a position where they reject any alternative viewpoint, or criticism of their own position, to one where they can evaluate different evidence and interpretations before reaching an informed verdict.

Several strategies can help pupils develop a more sophisticated approach:

- Debates are really useful tools, especially when you ask pupils to advocate an argument which they do not initially agree with.
- Similarly, the use of role-play can help pupils understand the perspective of different individuals.
- Encourage the pupils to brainstorm an issue in groups. This should allow them to experience different viewpoints in a smaller environment, where they may be more willing to take on board new ideas.
- Set groups a problem-solving exercise, where they have to use a problem–objective–solution–evaluation model. One exercise that

could lend itself to this type of activity is drawing the new map of the Middle East before the new state of Israel is created. This would open up a discussion on respective claims to territory, and, crucially, the evaluation phase would force pupils to reconsider whether their original objectives had been met. Hopefully, this problem-based approach might force those pupils who had very definitive opinions to think in a different way. The new National Curriculum places a much greater emphasis on pupils devising their own hypotheses, which are then to be tested in the light of a range of evidence. If a teacher could encourage a pupil to regard their initial position as a more of a hypothesis than a definite opinion, then there is a greater likelihood that that pupil's level of historical understanding will be enhanced.

◆ *The teacher needs to adopt a very clear role*

The role of the teacher is vital in ensuring the success of lessons dealing with controversial issues. However, much thought needs to be given to how that role is to be carried out. The teacher needs to consider the age and nature of the pupils, along with the type of issue being taught. There is a lot to be said for the teacher varying their approach across a series of lessons, as there is for seeking the pupils' opinions on how you should act.

In his research into delivering citizenship lessons, Doug Harwood (1997) identified six possible roles for teaching emotive and controversial issues in the classroom.

- Committed – the teacher is free to express his own opinions. Could this influence the nature of discussion?
- Objective – the teacher outlines all of the different viewpoints, but does not reveal his own.
- Devil's advocate – as a means of tackling preconceived ideas, or the emergence of a consensus early in the proceedings, the teacher adopts a contrasting position.
- Advocate – this role is designed to ensure pupils consider all viewpoints before making their decision. Combining the objective with the committed roles, the teacher outlines the different interpretations before providing their own opinion.
- Impartial chairperson – establishing a more pupil-centred focus, the teacher's role is restricted to ensuring all viewpoints are presented in pupil discussions, or through the presentation of a range of source material.
- Declared interest – with this role, the teacher presents his views at

the start of the enquiry, before outlining the alternative perspectives. In this way, pupils can identify teacher bias when making their own decisions.

◆ *Use a range of teaching techniques*

- Ensure that you create an exciting stimulus activity to draw the pupils in. Short video clips, or playing music, speeches, etc. as the pupils walk into the classroom can help engage the pupils.
- Use a good selection of visual material. Emotive images force pupils to go beyond their instinctive reaction, and lead them into creating their own questions about an event: why did this happen? Who was to blame? What the consequences of this event?
- Life graphs, attitude continuums and diamond ranking exercises are useful ways to explore values, perspectives and attitudes. As well as helping to develop the pupils' empathetic skills, they also develop all of the thinking skills prescribed in the National Curriculum: processing, reasoning, enquiry, creative thinking, and evaluation.
- Class debates, and group-based enquiries allow opportunity for discussion and listening to other interpretations.

Case studies

◆ *Teaching Irish history in Northern Ireland*

Whilst teaching Irish history in Northern Ireland is a very different experience than teaching it throughout the rest of the United Kingdom, there is a strong argument to be made that the experiences of teaching the province's recent past can be applied to the teaching of emotive and controversial issues throughout the rest of the UK.

History teachers in Northern Ireland are presented with a number of problems which their counterparts in the rest of the United Kingdom do not have to deal with.

The main issue is one of context. Simply driving around the province illustrates the very tight connection to past events which many people have, and the partial way in which it is viewed in different communities. The abundance of murals and street paintings reinforces the memory of past victories, heroes, betrayals and tragedies.

More closely than anywhere else in the UK, history is inextricably linked to identity, and therefore the formal teaching of the subject will always come up against strongly held community views on the past. As most schools in the province are still segregated along religious lines, it can therefore be even more challenging to present a range of interpretations to an audience which has had one particular narrative of the past drummed into them, whilst the pupils themselves may never have had much, if any, exposure to different communities.

Kitson and McCully (2005) discovered that anecdotal evidence that pupils struggle to shake off community-instilled attitudes is supported by qualitative analysis. Their survey of pupils across Northern Ireland suggested that some pupils were likely to use source material as further evidence to support their particular viewpoint, rather than using it to explore different interpretations of the past.

A further issue involves the attitude of teachers in Northern Irish schools. Kitson and McCully found some teachers reluctant to link the past to the present, preferring instead to avoid teaching any Irish history at all. These are described by Kitson and McCully as 'avoiders'. Another group of teachers, whom they categorize as 'containers', are willing to look at Irish history, but are unwilling to make any link to the present. They may well practise otherwise 'good' history, but feel unable to deal with the complexities and emotional involvement likely to arise when something more contemporary is examined.

Where both these two groups of teachers are concerned, the opportunities to discuss the origins of the recent conflict and to overcome misinformed viewpoints are wasted. In an interview with *The Guardian* in 2004, Kitson provided a further explanation why the conservatism of some teachers was regrettable: 'One of the most important roles of the history classroom can be to enable pupils to explore controversial issues in a safe environment' (Crow, 2004).

Without wishing to preach about this issue, there is a real danger that teachers who bypass controversial issues of this kind are making it very difficult for young people to build any common understanding of the recent past.

How then can Irish history be taught in Northern Ireland? The introduction of a common Northern Ireland history curriculum in 1991 was an important stage in providing a version of recent history not dictated by the attitudes of the community in which the school was based. In an attempt to overcome disputes over the narrative of recent Irish history, the emphasis was placed on history as a process of enquiry, with an additional aim of placing the problems of Ireland in a global context (Low-Beer, 1999). However, as the subject was not compulsory after KS3, pupils were not required to study the origins and development of the conflict.

However, recent changes to the curriculum, following the establishment of a more settled political consensus, should tackle both this problem, and the operation of an 'avoider' strategy. The revised Northern Ireland Curriculum stipulates that all pupils at KS3 should be taught to 'Investigate the long and short term causes and consequences of the partition of Ireland and how it has influenced Northern Ireland today including key events and turning points'.

The production of new teaching materials has provided further support to the teaching of Irish history. Teachers from across the cultural divide collaborated on textbooks which offered an evidence-based approach to aspects of Irish history. This approach did not omit controversial events, including sections on the Irish Rebellion of 1641 and 'Bloody Sunday' in 1972. However, its focus was not on what happened or on who was to blame, but on how reliable the various pieces of evidence were.

The use of an evidence-based approach is instructive as it forces pupils to keep a keen eye on the historical processes at work, and offers a model for teaching controversial issues in other areas. Examples of this approach are provided by the Ireland in Schools project at www.iisresource.org and include a programme of study, exercises and worksheets for teachers.

One of the best resources on the website looks at understanding entrenched political positions in Northern Ireland by examining the role of murals in forming identities and creating a version of the past which informs current attitudes. In doing so, it attempts to consider how different versions of the past have emerged, and invites pupils to comment on the messages, form and reliability of the murals (http://iisresource.org/Documents/0A4_HA_Con_Issues_Worksheets_A4_Sheets_pdf.pdf).

Much of the work on teaching controversial issues, such as the Troubles, assumes that teachers will only make links to the present day once the history has been covered. McCully et al. (2002) recount how one school in Northern Ireland has attempted to invert this process. The idea built upon the Speak Your Piece project, which considered how education and the creative arts could make a 'positive contribution in helping young people engage with controversial social, cultural, religious and political issues'. This project placed great emphasis on the need to take into account contemporary attitudes before embarking on a study of past events. As a result, it is hoped that young people will be able to make a tighter connection between what they study in the classroom and what they think about events 'in the real world'.

The history department at the school decided to use the BBC drama *Rebel Hearts* and feature film *Michael Collins* to teach the Easter Rising. Recognizing that the topic was likely to provoke a strong response from a predominantly Protestant pupil base, the department deployed the 'present to past to present' approach as a way of introducing the importance of context and bias when evaluating evidence and interpretations.

The first, and arguably most important, stage of the task explored reactions to *Rebel Hearts*, which attracted controversy from the unionist community primarily because of its author's alleged republican sympathies. Pupils were asked to evaluate responses from leading political figures and English and Irish newspapers, in order to recognize the importance of provenance.

The next stage was to compare how the drama and film dealt with key issues of the period, with the film representation of the same events, before considering which was the most useful source for studying the Easter Rising.

Pupil evaluations suggested that, on the whole, the exercise had been successful in making a link between the past and the issues of the present day, although there was some evidence of what Kinloch (2005) has referred to as the existence of two histories emerging for pupils; the history which they are able to perform in the classroom, and the history they receive and articulate in their respective communities.

◆ Teaching Islamic history

A number of historians have commented on the difficulties inherent in teaching Islamic history. The TEACH report highlights both the structural and practical difficulties, commenting on the dearth of options available at KS3, and the commonly held view that it is 'too difficult, alien or complex' to teach. Kinloch (2005) suggests that the nature of language used provides one difficulty for history teachers. Unlike most European histories, comparatively few Islamic histories have been translated into English.

Kinloch also identifies a more subtle problem: not all Muslims are happy for Islamic history to be taught by non-Muslims. For some Muslim scholars, the study of history cannot be divorced from its cultural and, especially, religious context. This represents a significant departure from the purpose and processes of Western history, and, Kinloch argues, Muslim historians therefore see the teaching of Islamic history as requiring a unique methodology. A second explanation for Muslim scepticism about non-Muslim approaches derives from a belief that Western historians will attempt to make their study conform to one of two distinct narratives. The first places the history of all developing countries exclusively in the context of Western colonialism, whilst the second dwells on Islam as the enemy of the West, stretching from the Crusades to the current 'war on terrorism'. As a result, teaching Islamic history may reinforce existing stereotypes and exaggerate elements of conflict.

Perhaps related to the above problems is the lack of available and suitable classroom resources. As most teachers tend to delve into Islamic history as part of a study of the Crusades, so most textbooks reflect this habit. As a result, there is the possibility that Islamic history will be dismissed as a sideshow to the study of a European campaign. This perhaps confirms the suspicions of those Muslim scholars who doubt the ability of Western historians to do justice to their history.

However, even spite of these obstacles, some of which are common to all emotive issues, there are ways to make the teaching of Islamic history both interesting and challenging. Both Kinloch and Ian Phillips (2008) argue that a prerequisite for the study of the Muslim world is the acquisition of sound specific subject knowledge. Fortunately, the development of new resources such as the Longman textbook *Meeting of Minds* (Counsell, et al., 2007) attempts to plug a sizeable whole in the market.

The book deals directly with Islamic history in its own right, rather than as an appendage to European history. Adopting an enquiry-based approach, it allows pupils to examine a world of important individuals and events without focusing on Western colonialism or conflict. In the process, it moves away from a singular focus on the Crusading era, and instead covers a very broad period of history, 590–1750.

Perhaps the most useful account of planning to teach the history of the Muslim world is provided by Alison Stephen, Head of History at Abraham Moss High School in north Manchester (Historical Association, 2007, p. 31). Whilst her account of teaching the Arab–Israeli conflict in a school where there is a 60% Muslim population provides a fascinating route through a cultural minefield, the four principles for planning a unit of work on Islamic history outlined in the TEACH report are perhaps even more useful to teachers embarking on a programme of study covering this subject area:

1. Focus on the positive aspects of Islamic history, such as major achievements and their significance.
2. Help students understand complexity, for example the divergent trends within Islam.
3. In common with other approaches to teaching emotive and controversial issues, great emphasis is placed on a critical treatment of evidence. In this way, pupils can move beyond any preconceptions about the past which they may have, and begin to understand the past from the perspective of different groups.
4. All debate and discussion should take place within a safe environment. As well of the ground rules laid down for the conduct of lessons within a classroom, public forums such as assemblies or school-based VLEs provide an opportunity for pupils to explore the varied angles of an issue in an environment where their views can be heard.

Tasks

1. Plan a scheme of work for the teaching of the Holocaust to Year 9 pupils. Consider what your main lines of enquiry are going to be, what source material you are going to present and the steps which you will take to ensure the programme is implemented successfully.
2. Reflect on areas of the curriculum where the issues raised in this chapter might apply. Do you think the TEACH report is comprehensive enough in its coverage of historical issues likely to prove emotive and controversial?

Developing students' interest in history outside the classroom

Young people learn better when they can get 'hands-on' experience for themselves. In so doing, they not only gain a better insight into what life would have been like for people in the past, but are also in a better position to make their own judgements on controversies and issues. One of the most important tasks for history teachers, therefore, is to convince their pupils that history is not confined to a textbook or classroom, and that historical processes can also occur in relation to museums, galleries and other sites of historical interest. Equally, these processes can be developed in imaginative and exciting ways outside of conventional lessons, but within the school context. This chapter seeks to explain how pupils' levels of historical understanding can be enhanced by developing their interest in the subject beyond the classroom.

Ways to develop pupils' interest in history outside the classroom

◆ History societies

One of the easiest and most rewarding ways to develop historical interest outside the classroom is to set up a History Society in the school. The very best societies are those which have a very high pupil input. Ideally, pupils should run the society, host its events, invite outside speakers, and give presentations themselves.

The focus of the society will depend on the age and needs of its members. In the sixth form, for example, a programme of lectures might be more appropriate to support their A-level work or prepare students for university applications.

The Historical Association runs an annual Great Debate competition for 16–19-year-olds, with regional heats taking place in schools. This type of exercise could provide a terrific opportunity for sixth-formers, and you could run your own heats through a school history society.

Lower down the school, you might want to provide a specific focus, such as investigating aspects of local history. Researching former members of the school who fought in the two world wars is often an interesting way to nurture an interest in local history whilst developing source skills and knowledge of the particular conflict.

◆ Working with other schools

An interesting and increasingly popular way to develop pupils' interest is through inter-school collaboration. With improvements in technology, pupils can even do this without leaving the comfort of their computer suite. Using video-conferencing or internet forums to debate historical issues enables pupils to develop their skills in a different context.

One idea for such a collaboration could be to model the causes of a major event, with different schools adopting the guise of different actors in the events of the period. The teacher constructs a series of scenarios, to which each of the 'actors' responds. This allows pupils to consolidate their subject knowledge and gain insight into different interpretations and attitudes.

An example of such an exercise targeted at sixth-form historians is provided in Figure 7.1. The reconstruction is set at the start of the Cold War, covering the period 1945–1949. The main enquiry is focused on who was to blame for the breakdown in superpower relations during that period.

◆ Visits

Sites such as castles, museums, houses and cemeteries are examples of the broad historical environment which can be accessed to develop pupils' level of historical understanding. Nothing compares to a visit to the actual site of a historical event, whether it is the beaches of Normandy or the iron foundries of Coalbrookdale. Topics which can appear dry can be brought to life, and pupils engaged by experiencing 'real' history for themselves. In Chapter 6, we deal with the importance of

Scenario 1 The war is nearing its end...the leaders of the three powers meet at Yalta to discuss what to do about the future of Europe

US position

Soviet response

US reply

Soviet reply

Scenario 2 Germany has been defeated. However, the three powers have to decide what to do about its future in post-war Europe

US position

Soviet response

US reply

Soviet reply

Scenario 3 November 1946: The Red Army remain in eastern Europe, and communist-dominated governments have been established in many of these states.

US position

Soviet response

US reply

Soviet reply

Scenario 4 June 1947: President Truman has announced his 'doctrine' and a programme of economic aid for Europe

US position

Soviet response

US reply

Soviet reply

Scenario 5 April 1948: unification of western zones of Germany

US position

Soviet response

US reply

Soviet reply

Figure 7.1 Suggestion for historical modelling task

creating empathy for figures in the past as a way of teaching emotive and controversial issues, and taking pupils out to sites of historical interest is a very useful strategy for helping young people gain a much better understanding of attitudes and feelings of people throughout history.

History visits do not even have to be extravagant or exotic, indeed some of the most useful are to locations which pupils pass on a regular basis in their own area. Whether it is a visit to a local war memorial, cemetery, National Trust property, air raid shelter, or statue, pupils can get a real feel for the historical environment and the varied ways that the past has been represented.

The remainder of this chapter dwells on the practical elements of constructing a school visit, and provides a selection of suggested visits to sites in the UK and beyond.

What steps need to be taken to ensure a successful visit?

◆ Learning points

- Ensure the relevance of the visit. History trips might appeal as a nice 'day out' from the classroom, but for pupils to gain much of value, the visits need to be fully integrated into a scheme of work, with a clear focus on historical skills. Planning for the visit therefore needs to be part of the planning for the year, whilst the processes at work will be of the same historical value as if in a classroom-based lesson.

- Incorporate planning for the visit into your teaching. Introduce the historical site into lessons, and discuss the purpose of the trip. The new National Curriculum includes historical enquiry as one of its three assessment strands, and you might wish the children to devise their own key questions, thus fulfilling the need 'to identify and investigate, individually and as part of a team, specific historical questions or issues, making and testing hypotheses'.

- Make a preliminary visit. Most museums and historical sites provide a complimentary visit for teachers planning to bring pupils. Use this opportunity to complete a risk assessment, and to evaluate how you are going to use the visit to inspire the pupils.

- As you would 'plan for progression' in the classroom, so you should do so on trips. The nature of the visit and the tasks which they carry out will need to be tailored to the needs of the pupils.

- Provide a variety of tasks to complete. If the pupils are walking round filling worksheets, they are going to get bored and will not get the opportunity to actually look at and reflect on the site they are visiting. Could you include tasks such as recording, comparing, filming, drawing, photographing, evaluating, interpreting? Figure 7.2 provides an example of a task which could be carried out during a visit to the battlefields of the First World War.
- Build on the work done during the visit in subsequent lessons. Avoid the temptation to set the pupils a project on the places they have visited, but instead use the sites as sources in themselves. Are they more useful than the sources in their textbooks? Do the sources they have seen agree with the interpretations presented in the books?

Cemeteries

You will visit cemeteries containing casualties from Britain, France and Germany. Each country has chosen to bury its fallen in a slightly different fashion, and accordingly the cemeteries prompt different responses in the people who visit them. For each of the three types, briefly record what impression you had of their atmosphere and design.

i   British (e.g. Tynecot, Ypres)

ii French (e.g. the Ossuary, Verdun)

iii German (e.g. Langemarck, Ypres)

Figure 7.2 Example task for pupils visiting the First World War battlefields

◆ *Health and safety*

Taking pupils out of school, particularly if the visit is a residential one or involves travelling abroad, is a risky venture, and one which places even more responsibility on the shoulders of teachers. Whilst serious accidents on trips tend to be rare, a number of high-profile cases in recent years have resulted in more stringent guidelines being implemented by the government. I outline below some of the things which teachers need to take into account before embarking on any school visit. Of course, *it is the responsibility of the individual teacher* to check with their own school or local authority what procedures and guidelines have to be followed.

Each of the teaching unions provides advice on all aspects of health and safety at work; the National Union of Teachers Health & Safety Briefing 2008 provides an overview of the main responsibilities expected of teachers taking pupils out of school, and can be found on the web at www.teachers.org.uk/node/66.

When planning a visit, teachers need to take into account the appropriate pupil to staff ratio. The Association of Teachers and Lecturers (ATL) recommends a ratio of 2:20 as an absolute minimum – this allows one teacher to remain with the group if the other teacher has to deal with an emergency or problem with a member of the group. For some potentially hazardous activities it may be 1:5, or 1:10 or 1:12. A judgement can only be made when all the risks have been assessed. Teachers should keep a written record of that assessment and the reasons for the final decision. ATL also advises, 'if in doubt, increase the number of adult supervisors' and in mixed groups have at least one male and one female teacher.

It is also essential for you to complete a school visit check list before the trip. Although this might appear to be a daunting and time-consuming task, it will, first, reduce the likelihood of as serious problem at a later stage in your planning, and second, help make your eventual visit an enjoyable and rewarding one.

The check list might include some or all of the following questions:

- Do you have the school's permission to take pupils on the trip?
- How many pupils and staff will you take? Have you recorded all details of your decision regarding staff–pupils ratios?
- Do you have medical and SEN information about each of the pupils on the trip? Have you liaised with the SENCO, school nurse and parents about these issues?
- Do you have the DCSF, local authority, school and other guidance on school trips? Do you need any further advice?
- Do you need to make a preliminary visit? Have you been before? Do you know anyone else who has been to the same place? Have you checked websites such as www.tripadvisor.com for guidance from previous visitors to the site? Will places of interest be open when you plan to visit?
- Have you done a risk assessment for all the activities? Does the site/venue have its own risk assessment? Do you need professional advice about any of the likely hazards?

- What are the travel arrangements? Have you done a risk assessment for them? Have you planned food and rest stops?
- Have you got parental consent for each child? Have you given parents all the essential information? What, if anything, do you need to know from the parents (such as emergency contact numbers, email addresses, medical, dietary details)?
- Do you have the telephone numbers and email addresses of parents? Do you have adequate insurance to cover the trip? Consult your local education authority for guidance in the first instance.
- Are the financial arrangements in order? What protection of payments is in place? Do you need advice?
- Have you adequate first aid provision? Who will provide the kit? Is there a trained first aider in the party? Do you have details of the nearest hospitals to the destination?
- What are the emergency procedures if anything should go wrong? Does everyone know them? Have they been understood and practised?

Suggestions for out-of-school visits

◆ *United Kingdom*

Imperial War Museum, London
The Imperial War Museum (IWM) is arguably the UK's most famous, and one of its most popular, museums. It is home to several permanent collections, covering the First and Second World Wars, the Holocaust, the 'secret war', and conflicts since 1945. The museum also contains an impressive gallery of war art, featuring work by Sir William Orpen, Sir John Lavery, Sir George Clausen, Augustus John, Sir Stanley Spencer, Paul and John Nash, Percy Wyndham Lewis, William Roberts, C.R.W. Nevinson and Eric Kennington.

Alongside the permanent exhibitions, the museum presents also special exhibitions, with recent presentations focusing on the art of the Holocaust and a study of children's experiences on the Home Front.

The IWM has also opened sites elsewhere in England, including the Cabinet War Rooms, HMS Belfast, Duxford air base, and, most recently IWM North at Salford Quays.

Links to National Curriculum Programme of Study: *The changing nature of conflict and cooperation between countries and peoples and its lasting impact on national, ethnic, racial, cultural or religious.*

Each of the examining boards offers a 'modern world' GCSE which will be relevant to the materials included in the IWM.

http://www.iwm.org.uk
Email: mail@iwm.org.uk
Tel.: (0)20 7416 5000

Manchester Museum of Science and Industry

Built on the site of the world's oldest surviving railway station, the museum offers a unique historical and cultural experience. Across its vast site, it features six main areas of interest: science and technology; industry and innovation; energy; transport; people; and communications. Whilst there is a distinctly Mancunian slant to some of the exhibitions, much of the material contained in the museum is concerned with the evolution of new technologies throughout the UK since the start of the Industrial Revolution.

Links to National Curriculum Programme of Study: *The development of trade, colonisation, industrialisation and technology, the British Empire.*

http://www.mosi.org.uk
Tel.: 0161 832 2244
Fax: 0161 833 1471

Welsh castles

Harlech Castle was built by Edward I between 1283 and 1290. It is a fine example of a concentric castle. It played a role in defending Edward's Welsh empire, and featured prominently in the Wars of the Roses and English Civil War.

http://www.harlech.com
Tel.: 01766 780552

Caernarfon Castle was built on the site of earlier Roman and Norman castles. Construction commenced in 1283 and continued until 1323, when work was brought to an end with parts of the castle still incomplete.

http://www.caernarfon-castle.co.uk/index.html
Tel.: 01286 677617

Conwy Castle is regarded by some as being the most impressive medieval structure on Europe, and has dominated the landscape since 1258.

http://www.conwy-castle.co.uk/

Pembroke Castle evolved from a Norman fort into a concentric masterpiece during the course of the twelfth century. It was later the birthplace of Henry VII.

http://www.pembroke-castle.co.uk/
Tel.: 01646 684585

Links to National Curriculum Programme of Study: *The different histories and changing relationships through time of the peoples of England, Ireland, Scotland and Wales.*

Maritime Museum, Liverpool
A great example of the local illustrating the national, this museum uses the experience of Liverpool's port to illustrate bigger issues such as slavery, the war at sea, the work of customs and excise and emigration to the USA.

http://www.liverpoolmuseums.org.uk/maritime/
Tel.: 0151 478 4499

Links to National Curriculum Programme of Study: *The development of trade, colonisation, industrialisation and technology, the British Empire; the impact through time of the movement and settlement of diverse peoples to, from and within the British Isles.*

Banqueting House, Whitehall
Built by James I in 1609, the Banqueting House is probably most famous for being the site of Charles I's execution in 1649, but it also offers fabulous architecture and the only surviving in-situ ceiling painting by Peter Paul Rubens.

http://www.hrp.org.uk/BanquetingHouse/
Tel.: 0844 482 7777

Links to National Curriculum Programme of Study: *The development of political power from the Middle Ages to the twentieth century; the different histories and changing relationships through time of the peoples of England, Ireland, Scotland and Wales.*

Hadrian's Wall
The Hadrian's Wall World Heritage Site stretches 150 miles from

South Shields to the Cumbrian coast, and features museums, remnants of forts, earthworks and parts of the original wall itself. If you plan to take a school party, you would be advised to select one of the 'frontier experiences' on the Hadrian's Wall website (http://www.hadrians-wall.org/plan_your_visit.aspx/Plan-Your-Visit), which provides advice on attractions around different sections of the wall.

Links to National Curriculum Programme of Study: *Links should be made to some of the parallel events, changes and developments in British, European and world history; the different histories and changing relationships through time of the peoples of England, Ireland, Scotland and Wales.*

Coalbrookdale

The Ironbridge Gorge museums at Coalbrookdale, another World Heritage Site, offer a number of sites which might interest students of eighteenth- and nineteenth-century Britain. Blists Hill is a recreated Victorian town, complete with authentic stores, a school and a pub! Drive past Abraham Darby III's iron bridge, constructed in 1779 and arrive at the Museum of Iron on the site of Abraham Darby I's original foundry.

> http://www.ironbridgeguide.info/
> Tel.: 01952 884391

Links to National Curriculum Programme of Study: *The development of trade, colonisation, industrialisation and technology the British Empire.*

Eden Camp

Sited on a former prisoner of war camp, it uses reconstructed scenes with movement, lighting, sound, smells, even smoke machines to present a realistic account of the Second World War experience.

> http://www.edencamp.co.uk/
> Tel.: 01653 697777
> Email: admin@edencamp.co.uk

Links to National Curriculum Programme of Study: *The changing nature of conflict and cooperation between countries and peoples and its lasting impact on national, ethnic, racial, cultural or religious issues.*

Dover Castle

Set high above Dover's famous white cliffs, its castle has enjoyed a rich and varied history. Visitors can discover clues as to its Roman and medieval history, whilst its role during the Second World War is explained through the Admiralty Walks, underground hospital and Admiral Ramsay's control rooms.

http://www.english-heritage.org.uk/daysout/properties/dover-castle/
Tel.: 01304 211067

Links to National Curriculum Programme of Study: *The development of political power from the Middle Ages to the twentieth century; the changing nature of conflict and cooperation between countries and peoples and its lasting impact on national, ethnic, racial, cultural or religious issues.*

Fountains Abbey

Currently owned by the National Trust, and given World Heritage Site status in 1987, Fountains Abbey was founded in 1132 by Benedictine monks, and dissolved by Henry VIII in 1539. It offers a well-structured programme of activities for pupils, providing sessions on *How did the medieval church affect people's lives?* and *When and why did religion first cause a problem for the Tudors?* Guides are provided by the Abbey, as well as resource packs for teachers.

http://www.nationaltrust.org.uk/main/w-vh/w-visits/w-findaplace/w-fountainsabbeyandstudleyroyalwatergarden/w-fountainsabbeyandstudleyroyalwatergarden-schools_teachers.htm
Tel.: 01765 643167

Links to National Curriculum Programme of Study: the way in which the lives, beliefs, ideas and attitudes of people in Britain have changed over time and the factors – such as technology, economic development, war, religion and culture – that have driven these changes.

◆ Europe

Many departments offer at least one overseas history trip per year. Faced with competition from other subjects, and a keen desire to bring the subject to life, many history teachers feel that there is enormous benefit to be had from short visits to Europe and further afield.

First World War battlefields

Probably the most popular European trip is to the battlefields of the Western Front. With the town of Ypres only 30 minutes from Calais, and the journey down to the Somme quite manageable in a day, schools can provide a fascinating trip for quite a reasonable cost.

Of course, most schools organize short trips to the Western Front primarily to support their teaching of the First World War either at KS3 or GCSE. However, for new teachers the prospect of building a trip from scratch is a daunting one. Whilst there are excellent guidebooks on the market, such as the Holts series, or the classic Coombs guide, to help visitors, I have provided an overview of a trip which I have run on many occasions. This contains an outline itinerary with brief notes on features of the visit.

As a battlefield trip of this kind is likely to feature at some point in a history teacher's career, I have provided a more detailed description of the main sites than for the other European sites which are dealt with later in the chapter.

Ypres

Possibly one of the most innovative and engaging museums on the Western Front, *In Flanders Fields Museum* (http://www.inflandersfields.be), approaches the study of the war from four angles. When you enter the museum you are given the identity of someone who would have lived or fought in the Salient. You then follow the progress of that individual throughout the war at several interactive stations throughout the galleries. The second theme covers the impact of the war on Ypres and the surrounding area. A broader history of the war is provided in the third section of the museum, whilst a selection of war art completes the final gallery.

Virtually every one of the 250,000 men who fell in the Salient would have left Ypres by the *Menin Gate* route. There was no gate standing there in 1914–1918, but the exit was flanked by two lions (now in Australia). The monument was designed by R. Blomfield and opened by Field Marshal Plumer in July 1927. It bears the names of 54,896 soldiers who died between 1914 and August 1917 and who have no known grave. Since 1929 (except 1940–1944), every evening at 8 p.m., the Last Post has been played in the gate.

It is possible to walk round the ramparts from the Menin Gate to the *Ramparts* cemetery. Many of the graves here date from the First Battle of Ypres in 1914. You will see the remains of concrete pill-boxes and emplacements.

The only really authentic sector of trenches remaining in the Salient, *Sanctuary Wood* is so called because when this was a relatively quiet sector in October 1914, stragglers were gathered together here and given a period of rest. The museum contains many artefacts of the fighting, but the wooden stereoscopic photograph viewers on the central table are particularly well worth looking at.

Tyne Cot (so named by the 50th Northumberland Division) lies just below the *Passchendaele* Ridge, 1 kilometre from the farthest point in Belgium reached by Allied forces. The Germans held the village until 6 November 1917. The Great Cross is built above the largest of the three German blockhouses. It contains the graves of 11,908 soldiers, whilst the wall behind holds the names of the 34,888 men killed in the Salient from August 1917 to the end of the war, but who have no known grave. Near the right-hand bunker are the graves of two holders of the Victoria Cross, Sergeant McGee and Captain Jeffries. Their exact location may be found by reference to the register in the gate house.

A very great contrast may be observed between the Allied cemeteries and the German *Langemarck Cemetery*. A mass grave of 24,834 men is approached through a red granite building. Beyond, over the far side of the cemetery, stand the brooding figures of mourning comrades. The cemetery is close to the site of the first gas attack of the war, in April 1915.

The forward base for the Ypres Salient from 1914, *Poperinghe* is surrounded by training camps, hospitals and depots. Many troops would come back to 'Pop' for rest and recreation during their time in the Salient. The home of Talbot House (Toc H) and Haig's headquarters for a time.

A series of cemeteries flank the road from Poperinge to Ypres. In one, New British Cemetery Brandhoek, lies Captain N.G. Chavasse who died in August 1917, the only man to win a Military Cross and two Victoria Crosses, the second posthumously. He was fatally wounded after an enemy shell hit his dugout. That same dugout contained several injured soldiers who had been rescued from the battlefield by Chavasse and other stretcher-bearers. Nearby, in Vlamertinge Cemetery, lies CSM John Skinner VC, DCM, of the King's Own Scottish Borderers, whose coffin was carried to his grave by six other holders of the Victoria Cross in March 1918.

Vimy Ridge

As you travel south from Lens, Vimy Ridge becomes increasingly clear. It also becomes clear why it was such a vital high point for the Germans to hold and for the Allies to take. The great barrier, rising 61 metres above the plain, protected an area of France in which mines and factories were in full production for Germany. The whole of the top of the hill is now the property of the Canadian government, and is a 240-acre memorial park.

A group of preserved trenches may be seen at Vimy. They have been reconstructed to show the front line before the ridge was taken. Look for pill-boxes, saps, duck boards, craters and trench mortars. However, the most interesting aspect of any visit to Vimy Ridge is the opportunity to visit the network of tunnels which were dug prior to the 1917 Offensive. The Memorial is on top of Hill 145, the highest point on the ridge, and contains the names of 11,285 Canadians who have no known grave.

The Somme

A series of cemeteries at *Serre* contain the bodies of the British and Empire soldiers killed in the most northern sector during the Somme Offensive in 1916. A short walk along a track that follows the course of 'No Man's Land' takes us to the site of the jumping-off trenches of the Accrington Pals on 1 July. The front line is marked by the edge of the wood where trenches can still be clearly seen.

Newfoundland Memorial Park, near Beaumont Hamel, is probably the most interesting place on the whole of the Western Front, and along with the Menin Gate, it receives the most visitors. It is a large expense of ground containing the complete trench systems of the July–November 1916 period, three cemeteries and three memorials. Newfoundland bought it after the war to provide a memorial for its volunteer battalion, which suffered so badly on the 1 July. A visitor centre traces the history and development of both Newfoundland and the Newfoundland Regiment.

Created by two huge charges of ammonal, two minutes before the start of the Somme Offensive on 1 July 1916, *Lochnagar Crater* measures 100 metres across and 30 metres deep.

The *Thiepval Memorial* designed by Lutyens was opened on 1 August 1932 and contains the names of 73,412 British and 830 South African troops who have no known grave. Behind the memorial are equal numbers of graves of French and British unknown soldiers. A new visitor centre was opened in 2004.

Situated in the southern sector of the Somme, the *Historial de la Grande Guerre*, Peronne, offers a fascinating overview of the fighting in that part of France. Hall 1 deals with events on the eve of the war in the principal nations of Europe, highlighting the sources of political tension and potential conflict and the formation of alliances. Hall 2 (1914–1916) covers the opening phases of the war from the mobilization to the German invasion and occupation of northern France. Hall 3 covers the period from 1917 to the Armistice, featuring propaganda, economic war, new weapons and the developing technology of war. Hall 4 covers the peace settlements. The Audiovisual Hall examines the Battle of the Somme as seen from contemporary documents and the testimony of a veteran of the British army. Finally, the Central Hall contains a collection of works by the German artist Otto Dix that brings home the meaning of war.

Verdun

In the three-and-a-half years between the Battle of the Marne, and Ludendorff's Offensive of March 1918, the German Army remained on the defensive behind an impregnable line. Only once did they come out from behind this line during this period. They did so at Verdun in February 1916, and almost succeeded in knocking France out of the war altogether.

Relatively few English schools visit Verdun, and those that do usually stay in Reims, about an hour away. After leaving the autoroute heading to Verdun, you join the road which was so critical in Petain's plan to keep the town alive: la voie sacrée.

The *Ossuary* at Douaumont was built between 1922 and 1932, and contains the remains of over 130,000 men, both French and German. In front of the building is a cemetery containing 15,000 graves, and to the left is a Jewish memorial. At the rear of the building it is possible to look through the ground-floor windows and view the bones of those unknown soldiers who died on the battlefield. Students can watch a short film about the battle in the basement.

On the north section of the Ravine de la Dame, only two men from the remaining seventy of 3 Company of the 137th Regiment were left alive after heavy bombardment during the night of 11–12 February 1916. However, no trace of the missing men could be found anywhere. It was only after the war that a clue to their whereabouts was discovered. The trench which they occupied, the *Trench of Bayonets*, was completely filled in, but remains of bayonets were found sticking in the ground. On excavation, a corpse was found beneath each rifle. It was therefore deduced that the men were buried alive during the bombardment whilst waiting to repel any German attack. Today a rather ugly concrete shelter, provided by an American benefactor, encloses the trench, and one bayonet can be seen protruding from the soil.

Fort Douaumont was the largest and most important of the series of forts built after 1871. It was equipped with flanking parapets, concrete casemates (2.50 metres thick), a 155 mm gun turret, a 75 mm gun turret, and two machine-gun turrets. Guided tours of the Fort are available, and visitors are able to walk round the impressive fortifications.

The village of *Fleury* was one of nine villages around Verdun that were obliterated during the war. Small white posts indicate the locations of the buildings that existed before the battle. On the site of the former railway station is the Memorial Museum of Verdun.

Normandy beaches

The Second World War is a popular topic at KS3, GCSE and post-16. With 50 miles of coastline to explore, five landing beaches, and a plethora of museums and attractions, the Normandy beaches offer students of the Second World War a huge choice of sites to visit. Some of the best include:

1. The Airborne Troops Museum at Saint-Mere-Église
2. Arromanches
3. Caen Memorial
4. Omaha Beach
5. Juno Beach Centre

Paris

In some ways the perfect city for a school visit, Paris has history, culture, architecture and is very accessible from the UK. Most schools include visits to Paris as part of an advanced study of seventeenth- or eighteenth-century France. Key sites of historical interest include:

1. The Palace of Versailles
2. Notre Dame cathedral
3. Hôtel des Invalides
4. Musée de l'Histoire de France
5. Conciergerie

Berlin

The proliferation of cheap flights to Berlin has meant that the city has become increasingly popular with GCSE and post-16 students looking to extend their knowledge of the Cold War and the Third Reich. Key places to visit include:

1. The Berlin Wall
2. The Reichstag
3. Potsdamer Platz
4. The Olympic Stadium
5. Museum Berlin-Karlshorst

Russia

Once the preserve of only the most adventurous of teachers, a visit to St Petersburg and Moscow has become a firm fixture in many history departments' GCSE and post-16 curricula. Offering a combination of tsarist and communist sites, and a wealth of art history, the two cities' highlights include:

1. The Hermitage (St Petersburg)
2. Peter and Paul Fortress (St Petersburg)
3. Museum of Political History (St Petersburg)
4. The Kremlin (Moscow)
5. Lenin's Mausoleum (Moscow)
6. Novodevichiy Convent and Cemetery (Moscow)

Tasks

1. Investigate sites close to your school. Assess how you could incorporate a visit into your KS3/KS4 programme of study. Design a set of resources to be used during the visit, with links to the key processes in the National Curriculum.
2. Design a modelling exercise which could be used within your school, or between schools. Decide on a main issue to investigate, such as the causes of the English Civil War, and a series of stages, where the different participants can give their opinion on events.

References

Assessment Reform Group (1999) *Beyond the Black Box*. Cambridge: Cambridge University Press.

Becta (2008) *Harnessing Technology Review 2008: The Role of Technology and its Impact on Education*. London: Becta.

Black, P. and Wiliam, D. (1998a) *Inside the Black Box: Raising Standards through Classroom Assessment*. London: King's College School of Education.

Black, P. and Wiliam, D. (1998b) Assessment and classroom learning. *Assessment in Education*, 5(1), 7–74.

Black, P. and Wiliam, D. (2002) *Working Inside the Black Box: Assessment for Learning in the Classroom*. London: Department of Education and Professional Studies, King's College.

Boice, R. (1996) *First-Order Principles for College Teachers: Ten Basic Ways to Improve the Teaching Process*. Bolton, MA: Anker Publishing.

Counsell, C. (1997) *Analytical and Discursive Writing at Key Stage 3*. London: Historical Association.

Counsell, C., Byrom, J. and Riley, M. (2007) *Meeting of Minds*. Harlow: Longman.

Counsell, C., Woolley, M., Chapman, A. and McConnell, T. (2008) Assessing differently. *Teaching History*, 131.

Crow, M. (2004) NI teachers 'avoid talk on the Troubles'. *The Guardian*, 11 September. http://www.guardian.co.uk/education/2004/sep/11/schools.northernireland.

Cunnah, W. (2000) History teaching, literacy and special needs. In J. Arthur and R. Phillips (eds) *Issues in History Teaching* (pp. 113–124). London: Routledge.

Department for Children, Schools and Families (2007) *New Arrivals Excellence Programme: Guidance*. London: DCSF.

Department for Children, Schools and Families (2008) *The Assessment for Learning Strategy*. Nottingham: DCSF. http://

publications.teachernet.gov.uk/default.aspx?PageFunction=-productdetails&PageMode=publications&ProductId=DCSF-00341-2008 (accessed April 2010).

Department of Education and Science (1985) *Education for All: The Report of the Committee of Inquiry into the Education of Children from Ethnic Minority Groups* (Chairman Lord Swann), Cmnd. 9453. London: HMSO.

Department for Education and Skills (2002) *Access and Engagement in History: Teaching Pupils for whom English is an Additional Language*, Ref. 0656/2002. London: DfES.

Eyre, D. (2006) Expertise in its development phase: planning for the needs of gifted adolescent historians. *Teaching History*, 124.

Fullard, G. and Dacey, K. (2008) Holistic assessment through speaking and listening: an experiment with causal reasoning and evidential thinking in Year 8. *Teaching History*, 131.

Garfield, S. (2002) From triumph to tragedy. *The Observer*, 13 October.

Harris, R. (2005) Does differentiation have to mean different? *Teaching History*, 118, 5–12.

Harris, R. and Haydn, T. (2008) Children's ideas about school history and why they matter. *Teaching History*, 132.

Harrison, C., Comber, C., Fisher, T., Haw, K., Lewin, C., Lunzer, E., McFarlane, A., Mavers, D., Scrimshaw, P., Somekh, B. and Watling, R. (2002) *The Impact of Information and Communication Technologies on Pupil Learning and Attainment*, ICT in Schools Research and Evaluation Series, No. 7. London: DES.

Harwood, D. (1997) *Global Express: Tune in to the News*. Manchester: DEP.

Hattie, J. (2008) *Visible Learning: A Synthesis of over 800 Meta-analyses Relating to Achievement*. Auckland: Routledge

Hay McBer (2000) Research into teacher effectiveness: a model of teacher effectiveness. Report to the Department for Education and Employment, June. http://www.teachernet.gov.uk/_doc/1487/haymcber.doc (accessed April 2010).

Haydn, T. (2002) Subject discipline dimensions of ICT and learning: History, a case study. *International Journal of Historical Learning, Teaching and Research*, 2(1).

Haydn, T., Arthur, J. and Hunt, M. (2001) *Learning to Teach History in the Secondary School*. Abingdon: Routledge Falmer.

Historical Association (2007) *Teaching Emotive and Controversial History 3–19: A Report from the Historical Association on the Challenges and Opportunities for Teaching Emotive and Controversial History 3–19*. London: Historical Association.

Historical Association (2009) *Findings from the Historical Association Survey of Secondary History Teachers*. London: Historical Association.

Husbands, C. (1996) *What is History Teaching?* Buckingham: Open University Press.

Husbands, C., Kitson, A. and Pendry, A. (2003) *Understanding History Teaching*. Maidenhead: Open University Press.

Kinloch, N. (2005) A need to know: Islamic history and the school curriculum. *Teaching History*, 120.

Kinloch, N., Kitson, A. and McConnell, T. (2005) Teaching controversial issues. *Teaching History*, 120.

Kitson, A. and McCully, A. (2005) 'You hear about it for real in school.' Avoiding, containing and risk-taking in the history classroom. *Teaching History*, 120, 32–37.

Laffin, D. (2009) 'If everyone's got to vote then, obviously ... everyone's got to think': Using remote voting to involve everyone in classroom thinking at AS and A2. *Teaching History*, 133.

Lee, P. and Shemilt, D. (2003) A scaffold, not a cage: Progression and progression models in history. *Teaching History*, 113.

Low-Beer, A. (1999) *Teaching Controversial and Sensitive Issues in History Education for Secondary Schools*. Strasbourg: Council of Europe.

Martin, D. (2008) What do you think? Using online forums to improve students' historical knowledge and understanding. *Teaching History*, 126.

McCully, A., Pilgrim, N., Sutherland, A. and McCinn, T. (2002) 'Don't worry Mr Trimble. We can handle it.' Balancing the rationale and the emotional in the teaching of contentious topics. *Teaching History*, 106.

National Academy for Gifted and Talented Youth (2005) *Supporting High Achievement in History: Conclusions of the NAGTY History Think Tank*. Warwick: NAGTY.

O'Grady, C (2000) Speaking in tongues. *Times Educational Supplement*, 27 October.

Ofsted (1998) *Review of Secondary Education in England, 1993 – 1997*. London: Ofsted.

Ofsted (2000) *Oftsed Subject Reports: Secondary History*. London: Ofsted.

Ofsted (2002) *History in Secondary Schools: Ofsted Subject Reports series 2001/02*. London: Ofsted.

Ofsted (2003) *Good Assessment in Secondary Schools*. London: Ofsted.

Ofsted (2004) *History in Secondary Schools*. London: Ofsted.

Ofsted (2007) *History in the Balance: History in English Schools 2003–07*. London: Ofsted.

Oxfam (2006) *Teaching Controversial Issues*. http://www.oxfam.org.uk/education/teachersupport/cpd/controversial/files/teaching_controversial_issues.pdf (accessed April 2010).

Phillips, R. (2002) *Reflective Teaching of History 11–18*. London: Continuum.

Phillips, R. (2008) *Teaching History: Developing as a Reflective Secondary Teacher*. London: Sage.

Prior, G. and Hall, L. (2004) *ICT in Schools Survey 2004: Findings from a Survey Conducted in Spring 2004*. London: DfES.

Prior, J. and John, P. (2000) From anecdote to argument: using the word processor to connect knowledge and opinion through revelatory writing. *Teaching History*, 101.

Qualifications and Curriculum Authority (2009) *Assessing Pupils' Progress*. http://www.sec-ed.co.uk/downloads/assessing_pupils.pdf (accessed April 2010).

Riley, M. (1997) Big stories and big pictures: Making outlines and overviews interesting. *Teaching History*, 88.

Roberts, C. (2005) English as an additional language. *Times Educational Supplement*, 23 September.

Scott-Baumann, A., Bloomfield, A. and Roughton, L. (1997) *Becoming a Secondary School Teacher*. London: Hodder & Stoughton.

Smith, N. (2008) Secondary history – zooming in on the past. *Times Educational Supplement*, 10 October.

Snape, D. and Allen, K. (2009) Challenging not balancing: developing Year 7's grasp of historical argument through online discussion and a virtual book. *Teaching History*, 133.

TES (2009) The seven secrets behind great teaching. *Times Educational Supplement*, 8 May.

Walsh, B. (1998) Why Gerry likes history now: the power of the word processor. *Teaching History*, 93.

Walsh, B. (2009), Stories and their sources: the need for historical thinking in an information age. *Teaching History*, 133.

Younger, M. and Warrington, M. (2005) *Raising Boys' Achievement in Secondary Schools: Issues, Dilemmas and Opportunities*. Maidenhead: Open University Press.

Resources

Quick glossary of terms

AfL	Assessment for learning.
AST	Advanced skills teacher.
Attainment targets	These define the knowledge, skills and level of understanding that pupils of different abilities and levels of maturity are expected to have by the end of each Key Stage.
BECTA	British Educational Communications and Technology agency: the UK government's leading Agency for information and communications technology (ICT) in education.
BT	Beginning teacher: a teacher who is working in a school as part of their initial teacher training (ITT).
CACHE	Council for awards in children's care and education.
CAL	Computer aided learning: applies to any learning experience that has been enhanced or supported by the use of computers.
CATs	Cognitive ability tests: an assessment of a range of reasoning skills.
CEDP	Career entry and development profile: used by all new teachers to chart their progression through their teaching career.
CPD	Continuing professional development.
CPO	Child protection officer.
Core subjects	English, maths and science: as part of the National Curriculum, all pupils must study these subjects up to Key Stage 4 (age 16).

CRB disclosure	Criminal records bureau disclosure: it is a legal requirement that all teachers are checked against CRB records to determine their suitability to work with young people.
Curriculum	The range and content of subjects taught within school.
DCSF	Department for Children, Schools and Families. Formerly known as the education and children's services department of the DfES. Government department that regulates all areas of education and the National Curriculum.
Differentiation	Differentiation involves teaching the same curriculum to students of all ranges and abilities using teaching strategies and resources to meet the varied needs of each individual.
DT	Design technology.
Diagnostic testing	A form of assessment that highlights specific areas of strength or weakness.
E2E	Entry to employment: schemes and training opportunities working in partnership with schools and local authorities to provide suitable life skills, education and training to pupils who may have been excluded or gained very few qualifications.
EAL	English as an additional language.
EAZs	Education action zones: based around primary and some secondary schools. Support can include: school-home support workers, extra-curricular activity centres, homework support groups in local libraries and so on.
EBD	Emotional and behavioural difficulties/disorder.
EdPsyc	Educational psychologist.
EMA	Education maintenance allowance: a fortnightly payment of up to £60 for students who are aged 16–19 who stay on in education after they reach the end of their compulsory schooling.
EMAG	The ethnic minority achievement grant: government money for supporting schools and local authorities to meet the educational needs of minority ethnic pupils.
ESOL	English for speakers of other languages.
EWO/ESW	Educational welfare officer/social worker: a

	person responsible for ensuring pupils' regular attendance at school and other related issues.
GCSE	General Certificate of Secondary Education: the national examination that students usually take in several subjects at age 16.
GNVQ	General national vocational qualification: courses in vocational subjects such as art and design, health and social care and so on.
G&T	Gifted and talented.
GTC	General teaching council.
GTTR	Graduate teacher training registry.
HMI	Her Majesty's Inspector of schools employed by Ofsted.
HoD	Head of department (sometimes known as head of subject).
HoY	Head of year (group).
ICT	Information and communications technology.
IEP	Individual education plan: a programme of support for pupils with a statement of special educational needs.
In loco parentis	Means 'in place of a parent'; the legal term defining teachers' responsibility for pupils in their care.
INSET	In-service education and training for school staff.
ITT	Initial teacher training: the period during which a teacher undertakes training to achieve qualified teacher status (QTS).
Key Stages	The National Curriculum is divided into four main stages:

	Key Stage 1	Key Stage 2	Key Stage 3	Key Stage 4
Age	5–7	7–11	11–14	14–16
Year groups	1–2	3–6	7–9	10–11

LA/LEA	Local authority/local education authority: a division of the local government with specific responsibility for education.
LSA and LST	Learning support assistant and learning support teacher: support staff for pupils with special educational needs, often works with individual children in class or within designated learning support units.
LSU	Learning support unit: a department within a

school set up to help students with learning and/or behavioural difficulties.

MFL   Modern foreign languages.

NT   National tests (formerly standard assessment tests SATs): tests used to show your child's progress compared with other children born in the same month. Tests taken at Key Stages 1, 2 and 3 cover the three core subjects; English, maths and science. GCSEs are taken at the end of KS4.

Key Stage	Age National Test taken	Published
1	7	No
2	11	Yes
3	14	No
4	16	Yes

NLS   National Literacy Strategy.

NNS   National Numeracy Strategy.

NQT   Newly qualified teacher: a person in his or her first year of teaching who has successfully completed their teacher training.

NRA   National record of achievement: a personalised folder detailing a student's achievement and attainment throughout their (secondary) school career.

Objectives   Goals, results or improvements that the decision maker wants to attain.

Ofsted   Office for Standards in Education: the organisation who is responsible for school inspections and assess the quality and standards of education.

PANDA   Performance and assessment: a report generated by Ofsted to allow schools to assess their performance and make comparisons with other schools nationally.

PAT   Pupil achievement tracker: a piece of diagnostic and analytical software produced by the DCSF/DfES to enable students' performance and attainment to be tracked.

Pedagogy   Refers to the art or science of teaching, but also describes the strategies, techniques and approaches that teachers can use to facilitate learning.

Performance tables	The collected statistics for schools and local authorities such as results of national examinations and absence data and so on, published by the DCSF.
PPA	Planning, preparation and assessment: at least 10 per cent of every teacher's timetable should be free for PPA time.
Programmes of study	The content of teaching programmes laid down in the National Curriculum for each subject.
PSE or PHSE	Personal and social education or personal, social and health education.
PSP	Personal support plan: personalised targets to support pupils often on the verge of exclusion
PTA	Parent/teacher association.
QCA	Qualifications and Curriculum Authority, the body that develops the curriculum and its assessment.
QTS	Qualified teacher status: qualification gained after successfully completing a period of teacher training needed to work in any state-maintained school.
SEN	Special educational needs: a term used to describe a range of conditions within three main categories: learning difficulties, behaviour difficulties or physical and medical difficulties.
SENCO	Special educational needs coordinator: the teacher with responsibility for SEN pupils within a school.
SMART targets	Specific, measurable, achievable, realistic and time-related: helping to monitor how targets and goals viewed and completed.
SLT	Senior leadership team.
SMT	Senior management team: the leading members of a school or education provider.
TDA	Teacher Development Agency, also know as Training and Development Agency for Schools (formerly the TTA – teacher training agency).
TLR	Teaching and learning responsibilities: responsibilities that impact positively on educational progress beyond the teacher's assigned role.
VAK	Visual, auditory and kinesthetic learning styles model refers to the preferred learning style of an individual and focuses on 'active' teaching and learning strategies.

Education and government

Department for Schools, Children and Families (DCSF)
⌨ Sanctuary Buildings, Great Smith Street, London SW1P 3BT
☎ 0870 000 2288   💻 www.dcsf.gov.uk

Department for Education in Northern Ireland
⌨ Rathgael House, Balloo Road, Bangor BT19 7PR
☎ 028 9127 9279   💻 www.deni.gov.uk

HM Inspectorate of Education (HMIE)
⌨ Denholm House, Almondvale Business Park, Almondvale Way, Livingston EH54 6GA
☎ 01506 600 200   💻 www.hmie.gov.uk

Office for Standards in Education, Children's Services and Skills (OfSTED)
⌨ Royal Exchange Buildings, St Ann's Square, Manchester M2 7LA
☎ 08456 404045   💻 www.ofsted.gov.uk

Scottish Executive Education Department
⌨ School Education, The Scottish Government, Victoria Quay, Edinburgh EH6 6QQ
☎ 0131 556 8400   💻 www.scotland.gov.uk/Topics/Education

Welsh Assembly Government Education and Skills
⌨ Minister for Children, Education, Lifelong Learning & Skills, Welsh Assembly Government, Cardiff Bay, Cardiff CF99 1NA
☎ 0845 010 3300   💻 New.wales.gov.uk/topics/educationand skills

What is a LA?
In England and Wales, local authorities (LAs) are responsible for managing all state schools within their area. Responsibilities include funding, allocation of places and teacher employment. You can locate your local authority via DSCF: www.schools-web.gov.uk/locate/management/lea/fylea

What are GTCs?
The General Teaching Councils are independent professional bodies with statutory power to advise the government on teaching. All qualified teachers in the UK working in state schools are required to register with a GTC.

GTC for England

☞ Whittington House, 19-30 Alfred Place, London WC1E 7EA

☎ 0870 001 0308   💻 www.gtce.org.uk

GTC for Northern Ireland

☞ 4th Floor Albany House, 73–75 Great Victoria Street, Belfast BT2 7AF

☎ 028 9033 3390   💻 www.gtcni.org.uk

GTC for Scotland

☞ Clerwood House, 96 Clermiston Road, Edinburgh EH12 6UT

☎ 0131 314 6000   💻 www.gtcs.org.uk

GTC for Wales

☞ 4th Floor, Southgate House, Wood Street, Cardiff CF10 1EW

☎ 029 20550350   💻 www.gtcw.org.uk

Teacher training

Administration

Graduate Teacher Training Registry (GTTR)

Responsible for processing applications for PGCE and PGDE courses in England and Wales, and Scotland.

☞ Rosehill, New Barn Lane, Cheltenham, Gloucestershire GL52 3LZ

☎ 0871 468 0469   💻 www.gttr.ac.uk

Training and Development Agency for Schools (TDA)

Government agency responsible for training and development of teaching workforce.

☞ 151 Buckingham Palace Road, London SW1W 9SZ

☎ 0845 6000 991   💻 www.tda.gov.uk

Training routes

Who needs QTS?

Anyone wishing to teach in a state school in England and Wales needs to achieve **Qualified teacher status (QTS)**. All the training routes shown lead to QTS or equivalent.

There is no QTS in Scotland, however, new teaching graduates are required to complete an induction year and register with the GTCS.

Bachelor of education (BEd)
An honours degree course in education. Courses enable students to study for their degree and complete initial teacher training at the same time. A popular choice in teaching primary school children: ⏲ 3–4 years.

Graduate teacher programme (GTP)
Trainees are employed by a school as unqualified teachers. On-the-job training is tailored to individual needs: ⏲ 1 year.

Postgraduate certificate in education (PGCE)
Trainees spend at least a third of their time studying at a higher education institution and two thirds on three or more teaching placements in local schools. Teaching placements usually last from two to seven weeks: ⏲ 1 year.

Postgraduate diploma of education (PGDE)
Similar to a PGCE, but followed by students in Scotland: ⏲ 1 year.

Registered teacher programme (RTP)
Training route for non-graduates, providing a blend of work-based teacher training and academic study, enabling trainees to complete their degree and qualify as a teacher at the same time: ⏲ 2 years.

School-centred initial teacher training (SCITT)
Trainees spend more time training in the classroom and are taught by experienced, practising teachers. Training is delivered by groups of neighbouring schools and colleges. May also lead to PGCE: ⏲ 1 year.

Teach First
Programme aimed to encourage top graduates to consider teaching as a career. Trainees work in challenging secondary schools receiving teacher and leadership training, as well as work experience with leading employers: ⏲ 2 years.

Pay and conditions

How does a new teacher's salary grow?
Newly qualified teachers are placed on the **main pay scale**

(salary scale for classroom teachers in Scotland) at a point dependent on relevant career experience. Salary increases by one increment each year subject to satisfactory performance.

England & Wales: main pay scale (From 1 September 2008)

Spine Point	Inner London	Outer London	Other
M1	£25,000	£24,000	£20,627
M2	£26,581	£25,487	£22,259
M3	£28,261	£27,065	£24,048
M4	£30,047	£28,741	£25,898
M5	£32,358	£31,178	£27,939
M6	£34,768	£33,554	£30,148

What is the STRB?

The **school teachers' review body (STRB)** reports to the Secretary of State for Education making recommendations on teachers' pay and conditions in England and Wales.

What about teachers in Northern Ireland?

Teachers' pay scales in Northern Ireland are generally the same as those in England and Wales.

Scotland: Salary scale for classroom teachers (From 1 April 2008)

Scale Point	Salary
0	£20,427
1	£24,501
2	£25,956
3	£27,432
4	£29,025
5	£30,864
6	£32,583

What happens when you reach the top of the scale?

In England and Wales, teachers who reach the top of the main pay scale can apply to cross the 'threshold' and move to the upper pay scale. In Scotland, teachers can apply to become chartered teachers when they reach the top of the salary scale.

Unions

Should I join a union?
Union membership is strongly recommended. Teaching is a demanding profession with many potential legal minefields. Teaching unions provide legal and professional advice, guidance and support.

What are the benefits of TUC affiliation?
Most unions are affiliated to the trades union congress (TUC) and members benefit from being part of a larger organisation. Independent unions typically cater for more specialised professions and are not bound by inter-union agreements or political affiliations.

Association of Teachers & Lecturers (ATL)
Represents teachers and lecturers in England, Wales and Northern Ireland. TUC affiliated.

▣ 7 Northumberland Street, London WC2N 5RD

☎ 020 7930 6441　　💻 www.atl.org.uk

👥 120,000

Educational Institute of Scotland (EIS)
Largest organisation of teachers and lecturers in Scotland. TUC affiliated.

▣ 46 Moray Place, Edinburgh EH3 6BH

☎ 0131 225 6244　　💻 www.eis.org.uk

👥 59,000

National Association of Headteachers (NAHT)
Main association representing the interests of headteachers. Independent.

▣ 1 Heath Square, Boltro Road, Haywards Heath, West Sussex RH16 1BL

☎ 01444 472472　　💻 www.naht.org.uk

👥 30,000

National Association of School Masters/Union of Women Teachers (NASUWT)
Only TUC affiliated teachers' union representing teachers and headteachers in all parts of the UK.

▣ Hillscourt Education Centre, Rose Hill, Rednal, Birmingham B45 8RS

☎ 0121 453 6150　　💻 www.nasuwt.org.uk

👥 250,000

National Union of Teachers (NUT)
Largest teaching union representing teachers and headteachers. TUC affiliated.
☒ Hamilton House, Mabledon Place, London WC1H 9BD
☎ 020 7388 6191   💻 www.teachers.org.uk
♟ 270,000

University and College Union (UCU)
Largest trade union and professional association for academics, lecturers, trainers, researchers and academic-related staff. TUC affiliated.
☒ 27 Britannia Street, London WC1X 9JP
☎ 020 7837 3636   💻 www.ucu.org.uk
♟ 120,000

Voice Formerly the Professional Association of Teachers (PAT)
Independent trade union representing teachers, headteachers, lecturers, teaching assistants, technicians, administrators and support staff, in the public and private sectors.
☒ 2 St James' Court, Friar Gate, Derby DE1 1BT
☎ 01332 372 337   💻 www.voicetheunion.org.uk
♟ 35,000

Curriculum qualifications

England, Wales & Northern Ireland
SAT	Statutory Assessment Tasks
GCSE	General Certificate of Secondary Education
BTEC	Business & Technician Education Council
NVQ	National Vocational Qualification
A Level	Advanced Level
A/S	Advanced Subsidiary Level

Scotland
Standard Grade	
Higher	
Advanced Higher	
SVQ	Scottish Vocational Qualification

NQF and SCQF

What is the NQF?
The **National Qualifications Framework (NQF)** and **Scottish Credit and Qualifications Framework (SCQF)** group together qualifications that place similar demands on learners.

NQF and SCQF equivalent qualifications

NQF Level	Qualifications	Vocational Qualifications
1	GCSE (grades D–G)	BTEC Introductory Diploma
		NVQ
2	GCSEs (grades A*–C)	BTEC First Diploma
		NVQ
3	A level	BTEC Diploma
	International Baccalaureate	BTEC National

SCQF Level	Qualification	Vocational Qualification
3	Foundation Standard Grade	
4	General Standard Grade	SVQ1
5	Credit Standard Grade	SVQ2
6	Higher	SVQ3
7	Advanced Higher	

Subject associations

Association for Science Education
College Lane, Hatfield, Hertfordshire AL10 9AA
☎ 01707 283000   www.ase.org.uk

Association for Teachers of Mathematics
Unit 7 Prime Industrial Park, Shaftesbury Street, Derby DE23 8YB
☎ 01332 346599   💻 www.atm.org.uk

Centre for Information on Language Teaching and Research
3rd Floor, 111 Westminster Bridge Road, London SE1 7HR
☎ 020 7379 5101   💻 www.cilt.org.uk

Economics and Business Studies Association (EBEA)
The Forum, 277 London Road, Burgess Hill RH15 9QU
☎ 01444 240150   💻 www.ebea.org.uk

Geographical Association
160 Solly Street, Sheffield S1 4BF
☎ 0114 296 0088   💻 www.geography.org.uk

Historical Association
59a Kennington Park Road, London SE11 4JH
☎ 020 7735 3901   💻 www.history.org.uk

National Association for Advisors and Inspectors in Design and Technology
▣ 68 Brookfield Crescent, Hampsthwaite, Harrogate, North Yorkshire HG3 2EE
☎ www.naaidt.org.uk

National Association for the Teaching of English (NATE)
▣ 50 Broadfield Road, Sheffield, South Yorkshire S8 OXJ
☎ 0114 255 5419   🖳 www.nate.org.uk

RE Today
▣ 1020 Bristol Road, Selly Oak, Birmingham B29 6LB
☎ 0121 472 4242   🖳 www.retoday.org.uk

Exam boards
Assessment & Qualifications Alliance (AQA)
▣ Guildford Office Stag Hill House, Guildford, Surrey GU2 7XJ
    Harrogate Office 31-33 Springfield Avenue, Harrogate, North Yorkshire HG1 2HW
    Manchester Office Devas Street, Manchester M15 6EX
☎ Guildford 01483 506 506
    Harrogate 01423 840 015
    Manchester 0161 953 1180 🖳 www.aqa.org.uk

Northern Ireland Council for the Curriculum, Examination and Assessment (CCEA)
▣ 29 Clarendon Road, Clarendon Dock, Belfast BT1 3BG
☎ 02890 261200   🖳 www.ccea.org.uk

City & Guilds
▣ 1 Giltspur Street, London EC1A 9DD
☎ 020 7294 2800   🖳 www.cityandguilds.com

Edexcel
▣ Edexcel Customer Service, One90 High Holborn, London WC1V 7BH.
☎ 0844 576 0025   🖳 www.edexcel.org.uk

London Chamber of Commerce and Industry Examinations Board (LCCIEB)
☎ 08707 202909   🖳 www.lccieb.com

Oxford, Cambridge and RSA Examinations (OCR)
▣ 1 Hills Road, Cambridge CB1 2EU
☎ 01223 553 998   🖳 www.ocr.org.uk

Scottish Qualifications Authority (SQA)
🖃 The Optima Building, 58 Robertson Street, Glasgow G2 8DQ
☎ 0845 279 1000   🖥 www.sqa.org.uk

Welsh Joint Education Committee (WJEC)
🖃 245 Western Avenue, Cardiff CF5 2YX
☎ 029 2026 5000   🖥 www.wjec.co.uk

Media

General media

BBC News	www.bbc.co.uk/learning/subjects/schools
Daily Telegraph	www.telegraph.co.uk/education
Guardian	education.guardian.co.uk
Independent	www.independent.co.uk/news/education
Times	www.timesonline.co.uk/tol/life_and_style/education
TES	www.tes.co.uk

Teachers TV

Freesat	650
Freeview	88
Sky	880
Tiscali TV	845
Virgin TV	240

Lesson planning

What is a learning style?

A learning style is the method of educating which best suits an individual. Teachers are encouraged to assess and adapt to the learning styles of their pupils. Common learning style definitions are shown below.

Auditory: learning occurs through hearing the spoken word.
Kinesthetic: learning occurs through doing and interacting.
Visual: learning occurs through looking at images, demonstrations and body language

Assessment

Formative
Teachers use their assessments (observation, homework, discussion etc) to adapt teaching and learning to meet student needs. Characterised as assessment for learning.

Summative
Students sit a test to assess their progress over a given period. Characterised as assessment of learning.

Inclusion – SEN and other barriers to learning

What do we mean by SEN pupils?
The DCSF defines students with **special educational needs (SEN)** as having 'learning difficulties or disabilities which make it harder for them to learn or access education than most other children of the same age'. School **special educational needs coordinators (SENCO)** are responsible for coordinating SEN provision within a school.

Attention deficit (hyperactivity) disorder (ADHD)
Students have difficulty focusing on a specific task. Easily distracted, they have a very short attention span and have trouble commencing work. Those with hyperactivity may act impulsively and erratically.

Autistic spectrum disorder (ASD)
Students share three main areas of difficulty: i) social communication; ii) social interaction; and iii) social imagination. The condition affects students in different ways, hence use of the word 'spectrum'.

Asperger's syndrome
Form of autism associated with more intellectually-able individuals.

Dyscalculia
Students have difficulty acquiring mathematical skills. They may have difficulty understanding simple number concepts and lack an intuitive grasp of numbers.

Dyslexia
Students have a marked and persistent difficulty in learning to read, write and spell. They may have poor reading comprehension, handwriting and punctuation skills.

Dyspraxia
Students are affected by an impairment or immaturity of the organisation of movement and often appear clumsy. They may have poor balance and coordination. Their articulation may also be immature and their language late to develop.

English as an additional language (EAL)/English as a secondary language (ESL)
Students whose main language at home (mother tongue) is a language other than English.

Emotional/behavioural disorder (EBD)
Students' behaviour provides a barrier to their learning despite implementation of effective school behaviour policy.

Hearing impairment (HI)
Students with a hearing impairment range from those with mild hearing loss to those who are profoundly deaf.

Individual education plan (IEP)
Document setting out additional support and strategies provided to meet the needs of a student with learning difficulties.

Moderate learning difficulty (MLD)
In comparison with their peers, students have much greater difficulty acquiring basic literacy and numeracy skills and in understanding concepts. Other difficulties include low self-esteem, low levels of concentration and underdeveloped social skills.

Multi-sensory impairment (MSI)
Students have a combination of visual and hearing difficulties. They may also have additional disabilities.

Physical disability (PD)
Students with a visual, mobility or orthopaedic impairment that impacts on their ability to access the curriculum.

Profound and multiple learning difficulty (PMLD)
In addition to very severe learning difficulties, students have other significant difficulties, such as physical disabilities, sensory impairment or a severe medical condition.

Severe learning difficulty (SLD)
Students have significant intellectual or cognitive impairments. This has a major effect on their ability to participate in the school curriculum without support.

Specific learning difficulty (SpLD)
Umbrella term used to cover a range of difficulties including dyslexia, dyscalculia and dyspraxia.

National SEN Associations

British Dyslexia Association
✉ Unit 8, Bracknell Beeches, Old Bracknell Lane, Bracknell RG12 7BW
☎ 0845 251 9002   www.bdadyslexia.org.uk

National Attention Deficit Disorder Information and Support Service
✉ P.O. Box 340 Edgware, Middlesex HA8 9HL
☎ 020 8952 2800   ⌨ www.addiss.co.uk

National Association for Language Development in the Curriculum
✉ Serif House, 10 Dudley Street, Luton LU2 0NT
☎ 01582 724724   ⌨ www.naldic.org.uk

National Autistic Society
✉ 393 City Road, London EC1V 1NG
☎ 020 7833 2299   ⌨ www.autism.org.uk

National Association for Special Educational Needs
✉ Nasen House, Amber Business Village, Amber Close, Amington, Tamworth, Staffordshire B77 4RP
☎ 01827 311500   ⌨ www.nasen.org.uk

Dyspraxia Foundation
✉ West Alley, Hitchin, Hertfordshire SG5 1EG
☎ 01462 454 986   ⌨ www.dyspraxiafoundation.org.uk

Royal National Institute for the Deaf
✉ 19-23 Featherstone Street, London EC1Y 8SL
☎ 0808 808 0123   ⌨ www.rnid.org.uk

Lesson plans

What should be included?

Many schools and universities have their own recommended lesson plan format. The suggested structure below provides a possible structure and key areas of content.

Teacher		Date		Subject	
Class		No. Pupils		Ability/Level	
		No. SEN Pupils		LSA Support	Y/N

Context	An introduction to… /Builds on material covered in a previous lesson… A cooperative/challenging class… strategies employed include …			
Aim	Why do we … What is the link between…			
Objectives	Understand key features of… Learn how to…			
Outcomes	Write down five facts about… Identify the key features of …		**Keywords**	
Structure		Teaching Activity	Pupil Activities	
	Starter		Work in pairs Recall previous lesson	
	Main Body		Complete exercise Work in pairs	
	Plenary		Write down Discuss	

Differentiation	Extension questions Peer support		
Assessment	Teacher led Q&A – targeted and open questions Marking books		
Resources	Text books, PowerPoint		
LSA Support	Focus on pupil x Circulate among all pupils		
SEN Pupils	**Name**	**Condition**	**Strategy**
		Dyslexia	Keywords on board LSA help writing h/w

Other useful websites

Site name: A to Z of School Leadership and Management
Description: Advice on legislation concerning schools, and guidance on a range of school-management issues.
URL: www.teachernet.gov.uk/atoz

Site name: Addresses of LAs in England with websites
Description: A comprehensive list of LA contacts, news, information and communications from the DCSF.
URL: www.dfes.gov.uk/localauthorities

Site name: Advanced Skills Teachers
Description: Information from Teachernet for teachers who wish to apply.
URL: www.teachernet.gov.uk/professionaldevelopment/opportunities/ast

Site name: BBC Key Stage 2 Revisewise bitesize revision
Description: Revision work for Key Stage 2 students in English, mathematics and science from the BBC Education website.
URL: www.bbc.co.uk/schools/revisewise

Site name: BECTA – British Educational Communities and Technology Agency
Description: The UK government's leading agency for information and communications technology (ICT) in education.
URL: www.becta.org.uk

Site name: Behaviour and Attendance
Description: Information about the government's programme to improve pupil   behaviour and attendance.
URL: www.dfes.gov.uk/behaviourandattendance/index.cfm

Site name: Birmingham Grid for Learning
Description: The public portal contains resources and links for learners, teachers, parents and administrators.
URL: www.bgfl.org/bgfl/

Site name: Building Bridges
Description: Information on the Independent/State School Partnerships Grant Scheme, set up to encourage collaborative working between independent and maintained schools.
URL: www.dfes.gov.uk/buildingbridges

Site name: CEGNET
Description: Careers education website from the Connexions Service National Unit for schools and colleges and their partners.
URL: www.cegnet.co.uk

Site name: Children and Young People's Unit
Description: The website of the government unit for the better coordination of policies and services for children.
URL: www.allchildrenni.gov.uk/

Site name: Choice
Description: First online course prospectus for 14- to 19-year-olds in London. Includes a free searchable directory of over 25,000 courses with clear details of all the learning opportunities open to young people.
URL: www.yourlondon.gov.uk/choice

Site name: Citizenship
Description: The DCSF citizenship website. Includes schemes of work and teaching resources, plus articles and information from assessment to whole-school issues.
URL: www.dfes.gov.uk/citizenship

Site name: Code of Practice on LA-School Relations
Description: Link to a downloadable version of the code, providing statutory guidance on how to raise standards.
URL: www.dfes.gov.uk/lea

Site name: Connecting Voices (COVO)
Description: A Southwark-based charity delivering services that address conflict, disaffection and underachievement in education and the workplace.
URL: www.covo.org.uk

Site name: Connexions
Description: Guidance and support for 13- to 19-year-olds in all areas of life.
URL: www.connexions.gov.uk

Site name: Curriculum Online
Description: A comprehensive catalogue of digital learning resources for the National Curriculum for England.
URL: www.curriculumonline.gov.uk

Site name: Don't Suffer in Silence
Description: Website showing pupils, their families and teachers how to tackle bullying problems.
URL: www.dfes.gov.uk/bullying

Site name: Education Protects
Description: A project funded by the DCSF aiming to help raise the educational achievements of children and young people in care.
URL: www.dfes.gov.uk/educationprotects

Site name: DCSF – Languages Strategy
Description: The Languages for Life website outlining the government's languages plans to transform language use and acquisition.
URL: www.dfes.gov.uk/ languagesstrategy/

Site name: Directgov
Description: Main portal for access to UK government services, including the latest, up-to-date public-service information.
URL: www.direct.gov.uk

Site name: Every Child Matters: Change for Children
Description: Useful materials and case studies to help understand and deliver the *Every Child Matters* agenda.
URL: www.everychildmatters.gov.uk

Site name: Fast Track
Description: Accelerated leadership development programme for new teachers.
URL: www.dfee.gov.uk/fasttrack

Site name: Global Gateway
Description: Information for the development of an international dimension in education. Including ideas for lesson plans, free downloadable resources, an area for young people and information on gap years.
URL: www.globalgateway.org

Site name: Go-Givers
Description: Site showing primary children what it means to be part of a caring society. Including case studies for assemblies, discussion activities and a range of resources ideal for teaching citizenship.
URL: www.gogivers.org

Site name: Homework: The Standards Site
Description: Support for the development of independent learning skills andattitudes for successful lifelong learning.
URL: www.standards.dfes.gov.uk/homework

Site name: Key Stage 3: The Standards Site
Description: Information on the KS3 curriculum standards.
URL: www.standards.dfee.gov.uk/keystage3

Site name: Learning and Skills Council
Description: Information and guidance on further education, work-based training, entry to employment and modern apprenticeships.
URL: www.lsc.gov.uk

Site name: Learning and Skills Development Agency
Description: National resource for the development of policy and practice in post-16 education and training.
URL: www.lsda.org.uk

Site name: LifeBytes
Description: Website for 11–14 year olds providing facts and information about their health.
URL: www.lifebytes.gov.uk

Site name: Literacy: The Standards Site
Description: Support for teachers and educational professionals to improve literacy in schools.
URL: www.standards.dfes.gov.uk/primary/literacy

Site name: National Vocational Qualifications
Description: Information on NVQs and the career opportunities they provide.
URL: www.dfes.gov.uk/nvq

Site name: Numeracy: The Standards Site
Description: Support for teachers and educational professionals to improve numeracy in schools.
URL: www.standards.dfes.gov.uk/primary/mathematics

Site name: Practical Research for Education
Description: Online journal for education students, teachers and education lecturers. Includes: free articles, profile interviews with researchers and a forum to discuss educational research.
URL: www.pre-online.co.uk

Site name: Primary National Strategy
Description: Support from the DCSF for all aspects of primary teaching.
URL: www.standards.dfes.gov.uk/primary

Site name: Qualifications and Curriculum Authority (QCA)
Description: Website of the QCA, the governing body who maintain and develop the school curriculum and assessments and accredit and monitor qualifications.
URL: www.qca.org.uk

Site name: School Lookup
Description: Access to the DCSF EduBase database of all nurseries, schools and colleges in the UK.
URL: www.easea.co.uk

Site name: SEN
Description: Special Educational Needs page from Teachernet offering information on SEN, including materials for teachers, parents and other education professionals.
URL: www.dfes.gov.uk/sen

Site name: Standards Site
Description: Internet materials and services aiming to support and improve teacher ability and raise levels of achievement.
URL: www.standards.dfes.gov.uk

Site name: Teachernet
Description: Education website for teachers and school managers, setting the government standard for UK teachers and schools-related professions.
Including resources, lesson plans and assessment strategies.
URL: www.teachernet.gov.uk/

Site name: Teachers' Pension Scheme
Description: Information about the Teachers' Pensions Scheme for England and Wales.
URL: www.teacherspensions.co.uk/

Site name: Teacher Xpress
Description: Resources and links to educational websites covering every area of the curriculum.
URL: www.teacherxpress.com

Site name:	Times Educational Supplement
Description:	Jobs, resources and ideas for all teachers and people working in education. Resource Bank section includes a large section of resources for teachers by teachers.
URL:	www.tes.co.uk

References

ATL	www.atl.org.uk
BBC.co.uk	www.bbc.co.uk/health/
British Dyslexia Association	www.bdadyslexia.org.uk
DCSF	www.dcsf.gov.uk
Directgov	www.direct.gov.uk
Educational Resources.co.uk	www.educationalresources.co.uk
GTC England	www.gtce.org.uk
GTC Northern Ireland	www.gtcni.org.uk
GTTR	www.gttr.ac.uk
Info Scotland: Teaching in Scotland	www.teachinginscotland.com
NASUWT	www.nasuwt.org.uk
National Autistic Society	www.autism.org.uk
NUT	www.teachers.org.uk
Scottish Credit and Qualifications Network	www.scqf.org.uk
Scottish Executive Education Department	www.scotland.gov.uk/Topics/Education
Teachernet	www.teachernet.gov.uk
EIS	www.eis.org.uk
TDA	www.tda.gov.uk
TUC	www.tuc.org.uk
UCU	www.ucu.org.uk
Voice	www.voicetheunion.org.uk

Index